THE HISTORY OF
THE MUSAR
MOVEMENT
1840-1945

by

LESTER SAMUEL ECKMAN

SHENGOLD PUBLISHERS, INC.

New York City

ISBN 0-88400-041-9
Library of Congress Catalog Card Number: 75-2649
Copyright © 1975 by Lester Samuel Eckman
All rights reserved
Published by Shengold Publishers, Inc.
45 W. 45th St., New York, N.Y. 10036

Printed in the United States of America

CONTENTS

In memory of my father Aryeh Lieb Eckman

INTRODUCTION

The Musar Movement took place amidst the uncompromising attitude of Rabbinism, the stagnation of Hasidism, the muckraking of the followers of the Haskalah (Enlightenment) toward Hasidism and traditional Judaism, and the barriers that historically separated the Russians from the Jews.

The founder of the movement was Rabbi Israel Salanter (1810-1883). When he arrived on the scene, nineteenth-century Lithuanian Jewry was in the throes of a profound religious upheaval: the spiritual wellsprings of Jewish life threatened to run dry. The Haskalah Movement aimed to reshape traditional Jewish life in the spirit of modern enlightenment, but its spread was largely due to a fatal weakness in the life of traditional Jewry itself. Torah observance still flourished, but it threatened to become a matter of habit and convention, without sufficient regard for the spiritual content of the law. Although some Jews were dedicated to the study of ethical works, unthinking observance represented a growing evil.

The Musar Movement was a protest against the inner life of Russian Jewry during the second half of the nineteenth century. Rabbi Isaac Blazer (1837-1907), an outstanding disciple of Rabbi Salanter, wrote:

> The fearing of God has immensely declined from a lofty position to a very pitiful, neglected, and hopeless stage; the ways of God-fearing are mournful; the houses of prayer are desolate; the sins increased beyond enumeration. . . .

The Musar Movement hastened to assume the responsibilities of once again raising the standards of learning, morality, and the observance of the laws of the Torah. It called for a spiritual and moral rebirth, a revitalization of the soul, an uprooting of distorted values, and the changing of the paths of life.

The movement merits a study because its participants were not only witnesses but also active contributors to the historical events of the time. The movement was concerned with the laxity of morality in the Jewish community, with the condition of the Jewish soldiers in the Tsarist Army, with the rise of the Haskalah, with Zionism, discrimination, problems of immigration, with religious and communal problems, and with the establishment of educational and rabbinical institutions.

The purpose of this study is to determine the impact of the Musar Movement from 1840 to 1945 on the moral, social, religious, educational, and political life of the Jews. It will emphasize the work of the movement's founder, Rabbi Salanter, and that of his key disciples, Rabbis Simhah Zissel, Isaac Blazer, Naphtali Amsterdam, Nathan Zvi Finkel, and Joseph Yozel Hurwitz.

Specific areas covered herein are: the causes for the emergence of the Musar Movement, its function in educational institutions both in the Diaspora and in Israel, the movement's part in relation to the military problems in the Jewish community, the attitude of the movement concerning the Enlightenment and Zionism, its dealings with Tsarist and Communist governments, and its role with regard to settlement in new lands.

There are no previous studies dealing with the Musar Movement in light of the Jewish and Eastern European history of the time. The existing material consists rather of books and articles dealing with the movement in relation to Rabbinic, Midrashic, and halakhic literature.

Rabbi Dov Katz's five-volume *Tenuath ha-Musar* attempts to trace the Musar Movement with emphasis on ethics, rabbinics, homilectics, and some primary historical information, for which the author of this work is grateful.

The author also gathered information from: the writings of the Musar Movement listed in section *A* of the bibliography; articles and letters compiled in the periodicals *Ha-Tzfira, Ha-Carmel, Ha-Magid, Ha-Lebanon, Ha-Peles,* and *Ha-Tvunah,* and in such primary sources as *Michtavei Hafets Hayyim, Or Israel,* and *Sichron Jacob,* listed in section *A*; interviews with former students and friends of the Musar Movement; general references of contemporary events during the movement, listed in section *B* of the bibliography; and the *Jewish Encyclopedia,* for the standard system of transliteration.

For the purpose of this study, the following delimitations are made. This study does not include an extensive investigation of the Musar Movement's writings dealing with Midrashic interpretations of the Hebrew Bible. The author does not include thorough research with regard to comments on the Talmud and the Code of Laws. He excludes from consideration popular articles on the subject which have no direct or immediate bearing on the themes of this study. The study is limited to published works, as well as published and unpublished letters.

May, 1975   L.S.

CHAPTER 1

THE TIMES OF THE MUSAR MOVEMENT

The Musar Movement took place during the momentous events that shaped the history of Eastern European Jewry during the period 1840-1945. The persecutions that became the avowed policy of the autocratic Tsarist governments in their treatment of the Jews naturally evoked a response in terms of ideology on the part of the oppressed Russian Jewish minority and on its leadership. The Musar Movement's reactions to these persecutions are especially interesting here.

"Musar" means moral or ethical. A carefully selected student body devoted most of its time to traditional Talmudic studies. In addition, however, the spiritual leader of the yeshiva (Talmudical school) delivered periodic "musar talks" such as the movement's founder, Rabbi Israel Salanter, had first introduced. The talks molded the character of the yeshiva student. These were not conventional lectures, but intense addresses meant to affect the listeners deeply and to create in them the longing for a life of self-improvement.[1]

Rabbinism and Hasidism

During the reign of Nicholas I (1825-1855) the followers of the movement witnessed the "rigid discipline" of Rabbinism on the one hand and the stagnation of Hasidism on the other. S. M. Dubnow, speaking of Rabbinism, writes:

> "And the ancient citadel, which had held out for thousands of years, stood firm again, while the defenders within her walls, in their endeavor to ward off the enemies' blows, had not only succeeded in covering up the breaches, but also barring the entrance of fresh air from without. . . ."[2]

---

[1]See Rabbi Dov Katz, *Tenuath ha-Musar* (Tel Aviv, Baitan ha-Sefer 1952), I, 21-53.
[2]S. M. Dubnow, *History of the Jews in Russia and Poland*, trans. I. Friedlaender (Philadelphia, Jewish Publication Society, 1916), II, IIIf.

9

Hasidic life, according to Dubnow, exhibited many examples of lofty idealism and moral purity. But hand in hand with this went

".... impenetrable gloom, boundless credulity, a passion for deifying men. ...."[3]

The Enlightenment's Efforts in Russia

The Haskalah, or Jewish Enlightenment movement, which began in the eighteenth century, was a part of the general Enlightenment taking place in Western Europe. Its adherents were known as Maskilim. The Maskilim set out to acclimate ghetto Jews to the ways of contemporary society educationally, socially, economically, and culturally.[4] Their purpose was to break through the seemingly

As far as the Russian masses were concerned, the Jews in their Pale of Settlement (enforced living areas) seemed as far away as China. By the same token, Russians living within the Pale did nothing to overcome age-old prejudices. Nikolai Gogol, in his novel *Taras Bulba,* portrays the Jew as an inhuman fiend whom the Russian masses should hate as an abomination of desolation.[5]

The Tsars and the "Jewish Problem"

Nicholas I had his own plans for attacking his "Jewish problem." He introduced the canton system—personal military service for his Jewish subjects. By doing this he intended to produce a new generation of "de-Judaized" Jews, Jews who would be completely assimilated and, if possible, converted to Christianity.[6]

He went further. He established "Crown schools"—special secular schools for Jewish youth which aimed to bring them "nearer to the Christian population and to eradicate the prejudices fostered impenetrable wall separating Jews from Russians.
in them by the study of the Talmud."[7] He issued a decree on April 20, 1843, for the eviction of all Jews living within fifty verst (1

---

[3]*Ibid.,* II, 124.

[4]See Jacob S. Raisin, *The Haskalah Movement in Russia* (Philadelphia, Jewish Publication Society, 1913). See also Salo Baron, *A Social and Religious History of the Jews* (New York, Columbia University Press, 1937), II, 213-224.

[5]S. M. Dubnow, *op. cit.,* II, 136f.

[6]See S. M. Dubnow, *Ibid.,* p. 15. See also Salo Baron, *The Russian Jew under Tsars and Soviets* (New York, The Macmillan Co., 1964), pp. 35-38.

[7]S. M. Dubnow, *op. cit.,* II, 58. See also chapter: *The Musar Movement and the Enlightenment.*

[8]S. M. Dubnow, *op. cit.,* II, 62.

Verst-0.6629 mile) along the Prussian and Austrian frontier.[8] Finally, in December, 1844, he issued a decree abolishing Jewish autonomy. He ordered

> ". . . the placing of the Jews in the cities and countries under the jurisdiction of the general (i.e., Russian) administration, with the abolition of the Kahals (Jewish communal organizations). By this decree all administrative functions of the Kahals were turned over to the police departments, and those of economic and fiscal character to the municipalities and town councils. . . ."[9]

Conscription Law

During the reign of Alexander II (1855-1881), the conscription law of January 1, 1874, was enacted.

Every able-bodied man at the age of twenty, without regard to his social status, had to enter the service. This meant six years in the active service, nine years in the reserves, and five years in the militia. Those in the Musar Movement were very much perturbed by this new recruiting ukase (imperial order). It threatened the very existence of the yeshivoth, since their students were among those being drafted. It was feared in the Jewish communities that the historic foundations of traditional Jewish life would crumble.[10]

May Laws

Oppression of the Jews in Russia continued apace under Alexander III (1881-1894), who enacted the May Laws of 1882. These laws prohibited Jews from settling anew outside of towns and villages. They suspended the completion of instruments of purchase of real property and merchandise in the name of Jews, outside of towns and townlets. The Jews were not permitted to do business on Sundays and Christian holidays. As a result of the stipulations of the May Laws, the Jews suffered economic hardships as well as overcrowding within the confines of the Pale of Settlement.[11]

---

[9]*Ibid.*, II, 59f.

[10]See Rabbi Israel Meir Kagan, *Michtavei Hafets Hayyim*, edited by Ariah Leib Kagan (New York, Saphrograph Co., 1953), p. 18. See also chapter: *The Musar Movement and the Jewish Soldier*.

[11]See S. M. Dubnow, *op. cit.*, II, 316. See also S. W. Baron, *op. cit.*, pp. 56, 57, 96, 261.

Nor was this all. In addition to the May Laws the government under Alexander III imposed upon the Jews a number of other prohibitions. Among these curbs was a *numerus clausus* for secondary schools and universities.

Under the pretext that Jewish students were quick to join the ranks of the revolutionary proletariat, a quota of ten percent was established, in 1887, for all such schools within the Jewish Pale of Settlement, five percent outside the pale, and three percent in St. Petersburg and Moscow. This was subsequently reduced to seven, three, and two percent respectively.[12]

The May Laws with all of their attendant restrictions stimulated the first large-scale emigration of Russian Jews to other countries, particularly to America. The Musar Movement was much concerned with the lot of Jews confronted with the hardships of readjustment in their new lands.[13]

The Decline of the Haskalah and the Advent of Zionism

The May Laws of Alexander III, in addition to precipitating mass emigrations of Jews from Russia, also resulted in the decline of the Haskalah Movement in Eastern Europe. The Haskalah in its deterioration was succeeded by two forms of secular Jewish nationalism: the Palestine-centered *Hoveve Zion* Movement in 1884[14] (this preceded Herzlian Zionism, which came in 1897),[15] and Simon

---

[12]See S. W. Baron, *op. cit.*, p. 57.

[13]See *Michtavei Hafets Hayyim op. cit.*, p. 54ff. See also *Sichron, Jacob* (Kovna, 1930), Vol. III. See also chapter: *The Musar Movement and Emigration.*
[14]*Hoveve Zion* (Lovers of Zion) was a movement of scattered societies that began to spring up in the 1860's. These groups gathered at a conference in Kattawitz, Silesia, in November, 1884, formed a federation, and elected Leo Pinsker (1821-1891) president. Their aim was to restore Jewish national life by colonizing Palestine. Their literature includes the following: Nahum Sokolow, *History of Zionism, 1800-1918*, with an introduction by A. J. Balfour (London, 1919), II, 281ff.; S. L. Citron, *Toldot Hibbat Zion* (Odessa, 1914), Vol. I; B. Dinaburg, *Hibbet Zion* (Tel Aviv, 1932), Vol. I. See also chapter: *The Musar Movement and Israel.*
[15]Theodor Herzl (1850-1904), as correspondent in Paris of the "Neue Freie Presse" was shocked by the impact of the Dreyfus case on the French people. In a spiritual turmoil, he grappled with the Jewish problem and arrived at a solution: the Jewish people must have a Jewish state. A "charter" for such a state in Palestine must be obtained from Turkey. A Jewish society must be organized to engineer the mass movement of the Jews to Palestine. A source of incomparable value on Herzl and his work are his *Tagebucher*, edited by Leon Kellner (Berlin, 1922-3), 3 vols., and his *Gessamelte Zionistische Werke* (Berlin, 1934), 5 vols. See also *A Jewish State*, translated by S. d'Avigdor, 2d. ed. revised with a foreword by Israel Cohen (London, 1934). See also chapter: *The Musar Movement and Israel.*

Dubnow's (1860-1941) Diaspora Nationalism[16] which was espoused by the Socialist Bund (1897). Both movements represented a revolutionary departure from the Orthodox Judaism[17] of Eastern European Jewry.

Zionism fostered the regeneration of Hebrew as the Jewish national language. Although Hebrew was indeed not spoken until the growth of modern Zionism in the nineteenth century, it had continued as the language of prayer and literature.[18] Diaspora Nationalism cultivated Yiddish, the vernacular spoken by German and Russian Jewry, as the medium for reaching the Jewish masses. The two viewpoints contended for supremacy in Eastern European Jewish life.[19]

Within two decades after its birth, political Zionism was accorded the recognition of the Western world in the Balfour Declaration (1917), which pledged British support to the Zionist hope for a Jewish homeland in Palestine. The Balfour Declaration states:

"His Majesty's Government view with favor the establishment in Palestine of a national home for the Jewish people,

---

[16]Russian Jewish historian Simon M. Dubnow developed his own interpretation of Jewish history, claiming that the Jews' unity and spiritual powers were preserved by the organized Jewish community during two thousand years of dispersion. He believed that Jewish unity did not depend upon a national territory nor upon an independent state. This unity, he felt, was kept alive by communal organizations, within whose framework Jewish culture and religion had continued their growth for two thousand years after the Jews' dispersion. Dubnow therefore believed in cultural autonomy and self-government for Jewish communities in Tsarist Russia and later in independent Poland. See S. M. Dubnow, *op. cit.*, II, 55-58; 131-142. See also S. M. Dubnow, *Nationalism and History: Essays on Old and New Judaism*, ed. with an introduction by Koppel S. Pinson (Philadelphia, 1968). See also S. W. Baron, *op. cit.*, pp. 168-172.

[17]The way of life that adheres to the traditional aspects of Judaism came to be called "Orthodox" in the nineteenth century, when Reform and Conservative Judaism, which differ somewhat from the original tradition, developed. Orthodox Jews continued to follow the laws, customs and ceremonies prescribed in the code of Jewish law. Orthodoxy long remained opposed to both socialism and Zionism, which advocated secularization of Jewish life. Many Orthodox Jews looked upon Zionism as the betrayal of the messianic idea (that the redemption of the Jews would come only after the coming of the Messiah). See S. W. Baron, *op. cit.*, p. 180. See also chapter: *The Musar Movement and Israel.*

[18]In the 1880's Eliezer ben Yehuda insisted that the Jews regain their homeland as well as their national language. His pioneering effort in the revival of Hebrew as a spoken language was taken up enthusiastically by many followers. See Nahum Sokolow, *op. cit.* I, 287; II, 284, 384 and his biography at the introduction of the tenth volume of his *Millon* (Dictionary) for more information on Yehuda and the Hebrew language.

[19]See S. W. Baron, *op. cit.*, pp. 158-181. See also S. M. Dubnow, *op. cit.*, III, 40-65.

and will use their best endeavors to facilitate the achievement of this object, it being clearly understood that nothing shall be done which may prejudice the civil and religious rights of existing non-Jewish communities in Palestine, or the rights and political status enjoyed by Jews in any other country. . . ."[20]

Dubnow's principles of Jewish cultural nationalism were incorporated in the Versailles Treaty[21] after the First World War and in the Jewish cultural and minority rights later granted to Polish, Lithuanian, Estonian, and Latvian Jewish communities.

Oppression Continues into the Twentieth Century

The first decades of the twentieth century brought to Russian Jewry a series of pogroms which revealed such bestiality as was not thought possible at that time. There were massacres in Kishinev in 1903,[22] in Bialystok in 1905,[23] and in other Russian cities and towns. The massacres led to an increased emigration from Russia, but at the same time gave rise to a Jewish self-defense body.[24] The misery of the Jews continued, in fact was intensified, during the First World War (1917-1921.) [25] The Bolshevik Revolution (1917-1921) [26] disrupted Jewish religious and communal life[27] and when, at the same time, Poland won its independence from Russia, Russian Jewry was split into two camps—one in Poland enjoying, at least in theory, varying degrees of religious, communal, and educational freedom; and the other in Russia, subjected to suppression on all of these fronts.[28]

Those who were involved in the Musar Movement witnessed these events. They contributed to various facets of Jewish communal life. The movement was concerned with building educational in-

---

[20]See Ismar Elbogen, *A Century of Jewish Life*, translated by Moses Hadas (Philadelphia, Jewish Publication Society, 1960), p. 478.

[21]*Ibid.*, pp. 502-509.

[22]See *American Jewish Year Book* (1903-1904), Vol. 5, pp. 19-22, 39, 109, 111, 112, 129-130, 133-141.

[23]*Ibid.*, (1906-1907), Vol. 8, pp. 36-37, 70-89.

[24]See S. M. Dubnow, *op. cit.*, III, 80, 87ff, 96, 116ff, 120, 129, 150, and Louis Greenberg, *The Jews in Russia* (New Haven, Yale University Press), II, 52, 54, 81, 155, 158.

[25]See chapter: *The Musar Movement and the Bolsheviks.*

[26]*Ibid.*

[27]*Ibid.*

[28]*Ibid.*

stitutions in the Diaspora as well as in Israel. It reacted to the rise of the Haskalah as well as to that of Zionism. It worked to help Jewish soldiers and immigrants. It fought the discrimination of the Tsarist Government against its Jewish subjects and later worked in behalf of Soviet Jewry. All of this will be discussed at length in succeeding chapters.

Chapter 2

THE MUSAR MOVEMENT

The purpose of this chapter is to determine the causes for the emergence of the Musar Movement, its goals, and the part played by its founder, Rabbi Israel Salanter.

The Musar Movement was a protest against the inner life of Russian Jewry during the second half of the nineteenth century. Rabbi Isaac Blazer, a prominent disciple of Rabbi Salanter, wrote:

> The fearing of God has immensely declined . . . slanderers have become powerful; men committed to resist sin are looked upon with disdain; wickedness prevails; falsehood will be clothed by the garment of righteousness . . . and justice is in a position of silence.[1]

Rabbi Blazer criticized the rabbis and learned men in the following manner: "Even in former years learning went hand in hand with God-fearing; and now the knot that tied learning with God-fearing has been severed; and God forbid, in the end, without God-fearing learning and practice of Torah will disappear."[2]

Rabbi Joshua Heller (1818-1880), another distinguished disciple, depicts the spiritual and moral life of the era in these words:

> The beauty of the Torah has become secular; deceit is the order of the day; greed for materialistic possession has increased; the love for pleasure has spread; haughtiness and grandeur in their search for honor will profane the teachings of God; the obligation of worship has degraded; passion is the ruler of the day; and destructive traits have been unleashed; and the little God-fearing and keeping of the Torah that are found, are kept habitually. . . .[3]

---

[1]Rabbi Isaac Blazer, *Or Israel* (Vilna, 1900), p. 4.
[2]*Ibid.*
[3]Rabbi Joshua Heller, *Dibre Joshua* (Vilna, 1966), Article I, Chapters I and II. See also Dov Katz, *Tenuath ha-Musar* (Tel Aviv, 1952), I, 59.

Rabbi Abraham Danzig (1748-1821), enumerates the evils of the era:

> There are bundles and bundles of sins that people are ac-
> customed to commit; among the most serious transgres-
> sions are slander, false testimony, insulting a friend in the
> presence of company and feeling haughty in doing it;
> causing suffering to fellow Jews with words and deeds; op-
> pressing the widow or the orphan; charging interest, hating
> one's fellow man, anger, arrogance, mocking. . . . The
> world is well prepared in carrying out the above evils;
> and even the most learned and prominent people if they
> carefully examine their hearts will find that the major-
> ity of them fail in morality by them.[4]

Rabbi Salanter was very much concerned with the laxity of the times regarding fulfilling the commands of the Torah:

> We witness that an individual refrains from committing
> many sins, even at a time when he is forced to transgress
> a precept by a circumstance. There are more serious trans-
> gressions than these that a person will be lax in abstaining
> from committing. An example is: a large portion of our
> brethren will not eat without washing the hands. . . . How-
> ever, in the case of slander, a grave sin, they will trespass
> easily. . . . Even the learned and almost the God-fearing,
> too, are lax in keeping the moral precepts of the Torah,
> which when they are transgressed the Day of Atonement
> and also death will not expiate them.[5]

Such were the conditions which caused the Musar Movement to emerge. The movement called for a spiritual and moral renaissance, a revitalization of the soul, an uprooting of distorted values, and the changing of the paths of life. It stressed the perfection of Torah, the perfection of deeds, and the wholeness of the person, so that an individual would be well adjusted to God and to his fellow man.

---

[4]Rabbi Abraham Danzig, *Chaye ha-Adam* (Vilna, 1936), p. 368.
[5]Rabbi Salanter, "Igeret ha-Musar" in *Or Israel,* edited by Isaac Blazer (Vilna, 1900), p. 106f.

Perfection of Torah

Jews must observe the commands between God and man and the precepts between man and his fellow man. Man must take seriously the laws and prohibitions pertaining to deed, thought, emotion, and limb. Just as people are careful in the observance of the Sabbath, keeping a kosher home, Passover, etc., so are they obligated to be wary of anger, slander, abusing another person, and bearing a grudge. A Jew is commanded to observe the precepts of prayer, and phylacteries, and at the same time heed the laws of "love thy neighbor," doing righteousness, and manifesting lovingkindness to the poor, the widow, and the orphan.[6]

Perfection of Deeds

The perfection of Torah should motivate a person to strive for the perfection of deeds. The Musar Movement called for deeds based on thought, feeling, and meaning. Prayer must be recited with devotion. *The meaning of a precept must be understood before it is carried out.*[7]

Wholeness of Man

Perfection of Torah and deeds should lead to the wholeness of the man. Character, good manners, and noble thoughts are of paramount importance in developing a personality well adjusted to God and to man.

In short, the perfection of Torah and deeds, and the wholeness of the person, which would help the individual to be well adjusted to God and to his fellow man, were the three pillars of the Musar Movement.[8]

---

[6]*Ibid.* See also Dov Katz, *op. cit.*, p. 60.

[7]"Even without knowledge and understanding we do recognize the belief that God is the Judge, to mete out to man his due, in accordance with his deeds. If his way of life be wicked and grievous he will be severely punished either in this world or in the world to come. . . . However, if his deeds are pure and upright, he will be called blessed and he will be recompensed with celestial pleasures in this world and even more so in the next." Rabbi Salanter, "Igeret ha-Musar," *op. cit.*, p. 103.

[8]"A man should devote himself to the duty of uplifting others, of arousing them to meditation on devotion and musar. Since man's eyes are open to the faults of others and he is aware of their imperfections, and realizes that they need ethical instruction considerably, he should therefore apply himself zealously to the study of musar, so that others may follow him, and fear of God will increase in this world, and he will be responsible for the merit of others. And in consequence, gradually the study of musar will lead one in the path of righteousness and correctness, the study of musar being both the physical and spiritual cure." *Ibid.*, p. 108.

The Founder of the Musar Movement—Rabbi Israel Salanter

Rabbi Israel ben Zeev-Wolf Lipkin (Libkin),[9] or Rabbi Israel
Salanter, as he was to become known to posterity, was born on November 3, 1810,[10] in the Lithuanian town of Zhagory[11] in the province of Samogitia[12] bordering on Courland (Livonia) and Prussia.
His father, Zeev-Wolf ben Aryeh Lippe, was a rabbi of renown, and
an author of "Marginal Notes of Ben Aryeh," which have been published in the Rome edition of the Talmud. Israel Salanter's first
teacher was his father, who introduced him to the study of Talmud.
From his mother, Leah,[13] famous for her charity and piety, he inherited his natural goodness, kindness, and simplicity.

Israel Salanter's father wanted him to be learned in Talmud,
not a master of mental Talmudic acrobatics, which was the prevalent
method of learning at that time in general and among the "wise
men of Zhagory"[14] in particular. He sent his son to study under
Rabbi Hirsch Braude and Rabbi Joseph Zundel. The former influenced his later life by emphasizing the mastery of Talmud. The latter
shaped him in the pathways of musar.

Rabbi Hirsch Braude was one of the keenest dialecticians
among the Talmudists of his time, famous for his intellect and his
rational way of thinking. Under his careful guidance Israel Salanter
learned to be thorough, yet not to use the hairsplitting type of logic
so popular at the time.[15]

In the Beth Midrash (house of study) Israel was inspired by
the humble and ethical behavior of Rabbi Zundel,[16] whose example
he began to follow. Rabbi Isaac Blazer wrote: "He began to enter
and leave [Rabbi Zundel's] home as his own son; concentrating to

---

[9]The name is spelled Libkin on the title page of Or Israel, op. cit.

[10]Emil Benjamin, pupil and biographer of Rabbi Salanter in his work Rabbi
Israel Salant, Sein Leben und Wirken (Berlin, 1899) is the first to mention Rabbi
Salanter's birth date as November 3, 1810. Dov Katz in Tenuath ha-Musar, op. cit.,
Vol. I, and Menahem G. Glenn in Israel Salanter (New York, 1953), also mention
November 3, 1810.

[11]Ibid.

[12]Known in Rabbinic literature as Zmudz.

[13]Israel Salanter's mother was well versed in the Bible and the Talmud. See
M. L. Lilienblum, Kol Kitvei, III, 42.

[14]Zhagory always boasted, and rightly so, of its scholars and "wise men." See
A. S. Sachs, Studies in Jewish Bibliography (New York, 1925), p. 23f.

[15]Menahem G. Glenn, Israel Salanter (New York, 1953), p. 11. See also Dov
Katz, op. cit., I, 139.

[16]Rabbi Isaac Blazer, Or Israel (Vilna, 1900), p. 30. See also M. G. Glenn,
op. cit., p. 11, and Dov Katz, op. cit., p. 142.

emulate his spiritual and ethical ways. When he walked in the forest to recite the words of reverence to God and of morality, Israel followed him secretly so as to understand and to absorb his sound words. . . ."[17] When Rabbi Zundel became aware that he was being followed he called to Israel and said, "Israel, study morality and be God-fearing."[18] His words so impressed Israel that he underwent a complete change. When he heard the voice of his teacher in the study of musar, "his heart was set aflame."[19]

From that time on, Israel Salanter devoted his time and energy to achieving high moral standards. He worked hard to attain his goals, and he soon became a symbol of moral perfection for his own and future generations.

He asked himself whether it was better to do good deeds covertly or overtly. He concluded that a man who is able to influence others should not withdraw from society. He believed that man was born not for himself but for others, and so was obligated to help others as much as possible.[20]

He derided the many learned Talmudical scholars who "hibernated" in their rooms, doing nothing to educate and strengthen the morale of the masses. He found that these same masses led lives without meaning, and that they longed to improve their condition educationally, economically, and spiritually.[21]

He felt that men were guided by habit and passion. He observed that the portions of the Torah dealing with ethics and morals between man and his fellow man were neglected.[22] He set out to change the habits of Jewish society through morality.

Rabbi Salanter knew that the Rabbinic scholars of the day, and the common man as well, admired an outstanding Talmudist trained in the dialectic method. He himself was reluctant at first to appear as an authority on the Talmud or as an expert in the dialectic method. However, he changed his mind, and soon began to travel to cities and towns to lecture on the Talmud and musar—according to dialectics. He was welcome everywhere, and was recognized as a great Talmudical authority. His speeches were emo-

---

[17]See Rabbi Isaac Blazer, *op. cit.*, p. 124
[18]*Ibid.*, p. 124.
[19]*Ibid.*
[20]Rabbi Isaac Blazer, *op. cit.*, p. 111.
[21]Dov Katz, *op. cit.*, p. 145.
[22]*Ibid.*

tional, touching the hearts of the people and bringing them closer to reverence for God.[23] He refused to take a pulpit, but happily accepted the appointment of dean of a seminary in Vilna in 1840.

Rabbi Salanter astonished the learned men of Vilna with his brilliance and dialectics.[24] He was determined to begin in Vilna the arduous task of spreading morality. He assembled people in study houses and lectured to them on reverence for God.

At this period of time, sermons were not usually given by the rabbis. Those who did try to deliver them were not at all skilled in this art. Rabbi Salanter can be considered an innovator in sermon delivery. He was well versed in every aspect of Jewish life, and could touch the heart of an erudite rabbi as well as that of a coach-driver. His gift of speech enabled the sermon to regain its former status. His students were superbly trained in sermon delivery.[25]

The first musar study house was set up on the property of Rabbi Zalman ben Rabbi Uria. Rabbi Salanter visited the study house frequently, discussing with the people the topic of "giving account of the soul," the method of spreading musar, and reverence. In the "house for musar" Rabbi Salanter introduced the moral conversation.[26] The participants were so moved by his discussion that at times they were driven into an ecstasy, shouting in prayer to God for revitalization of the soul and purity of thought and heart.

Rabbi Salanter was very much concerned with the dissemination of books dealing with morality. In 1844 he worked arduously to publish the following books: *Path of the Righteous* by Haim Luzzatto and *Giving Account of the Soul* by Mantel Lefen of Stanov. In 1845, *Correction of Attributes of the Soul*, by Shlomo ben Gabirol, was published.[27]

In 1848, Rabbi Salanter interrupted his discourses on musar to help alleviate the misery of his people. Epidemics of plague and cholera spread in Vilna, causing many deaths. Rabbi Salanter was convinced that every Jew, in particular every man of the Talmud, was obligated to lend a helping hand to the sick, so that lives might

---

[23]*Ibid.*
[24]*Ibid.*, p. 148.
[25]*Ibid.*, p. 152f.
[26]*Ibid.*, p. 154.
[27]*Ibid.*, p. 155.

be saved. He himself assumed the leadership in Vilna for setting up relief work.[28]

The followers of the Enlightenment in Vilna heard of Rabbi Salanter's ideas of revitalization of Judaism. They felt that he was not opposed to them in their attempt to bring the beauty of the European Enlightenment to Vilna. They approached him. They informed him that their goal— bringing a moral and spiritual renaissance to Judaism—was similar to his, and that they were ready to help him in spreading his ideas.[29]

In 1848 the Rabbinical Seminary of Vilna was established and Adam Cohen was named chairman of Judaic studies. The Maskilim, however, thought the seminary needed a distinguished Talmudical scholar at its head in order to gain recognition and acclaim. They felt that Rabbi Salanter was the most fitting person for this appointment and so they offered it to him, at a salary of eight hundred rubles a year. This was an exorbitant amount of money in those times. However, Rabbi Salanter shared the view of contemporary rabbis that this seminary would be a liability rather than an asset to Judaism, and he turned the offer down,[30] whereupon the Maskilim invited Russian Minister of Education Count S.S. Uvarov to "persuade" him. When Rabbi Salanter realized that the Tsarist Government was pressing him to accept the deanship of the seminary, he left Vilna.[31]

Rabbi Salanter understood the motives of the Tsarist Government in establishing rabbinical seminaries in Vilna and Zhitomir. Nicholas I wanted to make changes in traditional Judaism along the lines of Reform Judaism (as practiced in Germany), and to encourage assimilation and conversion. In time everyone became convinced of this. Many students in the rabbinical seminaries of Vilna and Zhitomir rebelled against traditional Judaism and mocked its rituals, and indeed some of them did convert to Russian Orthodoxy.

Rabbi Salanter left Vilna in 1849, and settled in Kovna. He kept in touch with his students in Vilna through letters, in which

---

[28]*Ibid.*, pp. 156-162. See also *Or Israel, op. cit.*, p. 5 and Jacob Lipschitz, *Sichron Jacob*, II, 176-177.

[29]*Ibid.*, p. 163.

[30]*Ibid.*, p. 163. See also Jacob Lipschitz, *Sichron Jacob* II, 176 and Emil Benjamin, *op. cit.* 10.

[31]*Ibid.*, p. 164.

he related his views on morality and in which he encouraged them to follow its practice. With the support of the communal leader of Kovna, Zvi Neveizer, he set up a seminary there for the spreading of Judaism and morality. In Vilna, Rabbi Salanter had been engrossed in spreading Torah and musar to adults, while in Kovna, young students were his primary concern. He hoped that from the young students there would emerge a generation well versed in Torah, imbued with musar, and well adjusted to God and humanity. He wanted to set a precedent in the study of Torah and musar and to raise standards of learning as high as possible. He taught morality with an emotional appeal.[32]

After nine successful years in Kovna Rabbi Salanter went to Germany, there to revitalize the practice of traditional Judaism. Reform Judaism, secular education, and assimilation were the order of the day in Germany. Since Germany was the home of the Enlightenment, and since the Enlightenment had started to spread as far as Russia, Rabbi Salanter decided to wage war against the ideas of assimilation and Reform Judaism in their birthplace. In Germany he also saw the opportunity to inculcate Judaism and morality into college-educated men.[33]

From 1845 to 1849 he established, with the help of his students, houses of study for workers in many of the cities of Lithuania and Germany. In 1877 he established an academy for higher Jewish learning in Kovna, geared to serve married students who wanted to pursue their studies. The aim of this school was to produce expert teachers.

Rabbi Israel Salanter has left for historians a record of political and communal accomplishment. In Kovna, he was interested not only in the spiritual welfare of the Jews but also in the social, political, and economic problems of his brethren. Rabbi Jacob Lipschitz, an active participant in the communal affairs of his time, tells us of Rabbi Salanter's interest in communal problems in his book *Sichron Jacob* (*Remembrance of Jacob*).

The Tsars inflicted upon the Jews the conscription system, the expulsion of the Jews from the Grodno villages, the banishment of Jews from Kiev, and the confinement of the Jews within the Pale of Settlement. Rabbi Salanter felt that he had an obligation to his

---

[32]*Ibid.*, p. 170.
[33]*Ibid.*, pp. 181-187.

fellow Jews to help abrogate the harsh decrees, or at least to lessen their cruelty. He organized a committee made up of his students and friends, who devoted their energy to find solutions to the hardships of the Jews.

With all of this, Rabbi Salanter was still convinced, until the day he died, that because of his own personal shortcomings he had not merited success in his mission of spreading Torah and morality. In 1880, at the age of seventy, he set out on one more errand in the divine service. He made a trip to Paris to bring badly-needed spiritual leadership to the Russian-Jewish colony there. Shortly after his return, on the twenty-fifth day of Shevat (February), 1883, he passed away in the city of Koenigsberg, believing himself a failure and unaware that the seminary for married students in Kovna was only the first of a large number of yeshivoth that would, in time, carry the message of musar around the world.

CHAPTER 3

THE MUSAR MOVEMENT'S RELATIONSHIP
TO THE ENLIGHTENMENT

The Attitude toward Government-Sponsored Seminaries

In 1847 the Russian Government opened up two rabbinical seminaries, one in Vilna and the other in Zhitomir, which taught secular and Judaic studies. The city of Vilna[1] was the center of the Haskalah in Lithuania and the home of such prominent writers as Mordecai Aaron Ginzburg (1796-1846),[2] the poet Abraham Baer Lebensohn (1794-1878),[3] and others. Among them were religious followers of the Haskalah who strived to bring Judaism to its former citadel by combining religious learning with secular knowledge.

Rabbi Salanter and his followers were aware of the German Haskalah and felt that the Maskilim of Vilna were influenced by it.[4] Just as the Haskalah of Germany led to assimilation, conversion of many Jews, and a distortion of traditional Judaism, so, Rabbi Salanter felt, would the Enlightenment in Vilna bring the same consequences in Lithuania.[5] Rabbi Salanter and his followers were convinced that the Russian Government wanted to force assimilation upon religious Jews by instituting secular studies in the rabbinical seminaries of Vilna and Zhitomir. They felt that these seminaries would not produce outstanding scholars of the Talmud and persons dedicated with all their hearts to God and Judaism. They objected violently to these seminaries, causing a rift between the rabbis and the followers of the Haskalah.[6]

The Vilna circle of Maskilim, to gain recognition, sought a

---

[1]For more information on the city of Vilna at this time see S. J. Fuenn, *Kirmah Nemana;* and also the letter from Rabbi Isaac ben Jacob to Isaac Lebensohn, August 28, 1855, which can be found in *ha-Kerem,* 1888, pp. 58-59.

[2]For information on the life and works of Mordecai Ginzburg see Joseph Klausner, *Historia Shel ha-Sifruth ha-Ivrith ha-Hadassah* (Jerusalem, 1954), I, pp. 270-287.

[3]*Ibid.,* pp. 287-305.

[4]Jacob Lipschitz, *Sichron Jacob* (Kovna, 1927), II, 18ff. See also Dov Katz, *Tenuath ha-Musar* (Tel Aviv, 1968), I, 162f.

[5]*Ibid.*

[6]See chapter: *The Musar Movement.*

distinguished scholar as its leader, as well as brilliant students. We have seen how Rabbi Salanter left Vilna rather than head its seminary. The Maskilim also attempted to persuade Rabbi Israel Meir Kagan (1838-1933) [7] to enroll there as a student. A. B. Lebensohn, one of the founders of the Haskalah Movement, had heard about the brilliant young Talmudist from Radun, and made an effort to entice him into the circle. Rabbi Kagan, however, had been influenced by the moral teachings of Rabbi Salanter. He "rejected the flattering attention paid to him and the offers of a moneyed future; he determined to proceed with the pure course of the Torah. . . ."[8] Rabbi Salanter and Rabbi Kagan saw in the Haskalah a force designed to destroy the authority of the rabbis and to undermine traditional Judaism. They were convinced that Tsar Nicholas I was using the Enlightenment as an instrument to bring about Jewish assimilation. Their conviction was verified by the insulting declarations of Russian Minister of Education Uvarov:

> The best among the Jews are conscious of the fact that one
> of the principal causes of their humiliation lies in the per-
> verted interpretation of their religious traditions, that . . .
> the Talmud demoralized and continues to demoralize their
> coreligionists. But nowhere is the influence of the Talmud
> so potent as among us and in the kingdom of Poland. This
> influence can be counteracted only by the Enlightenment,
> and the Government can do no better than to act in
> the spirit that animates the handful of the best among
> them. . . .[9]

The Failure of the Seminaries

The Tsarist Government closed the rabbinical seminaries in Vilna and Zhitomir in 1873, after they had been functioning for about a quarter of a century. These schools failed not only the Orthodox Jews in Russia, but the government as well. In 1882,

---

[7] Rabbi Kagan is also known by the name "Hafets Hayyim" after the title of his book *Hafets Hayyim* (1873).

[8] H. M. Yosher, "Israel Meir ha-Kohen—Hafets Hayyim"; *Jewish Leaders*, edited by Leo Jung (Jerusalem, 1964), p. 461. See also Dov Katz, *Tenuath ha-Musar* (Tel Aviv, 1963), IV, 21f.

[9] S. M. Dubnow, *History of the Jews in Russia and Poland* (Philadelphia, 1946), II, 51.

Rabbi Isaac Elhanan received a copy of a proposition that young Baron David Gunzburg, with the consent of his father, Baron Horace Gunzburg, had sent to the Superintendent of Education in Vilna, to reopen the rabbinical seminary of Vilna. The Orthodox Jews were indignant that so young a man as Baron Gunzburg, should, by himself, seek to reopen a seminary that had proved as detrimental to Judaism as it was unsuccessful.[10] Rabbi Salanter and Rabbi Elhanan opposed the Gunzburg proposition. However, Rabbi Salanter prevailed upon Rabbi Jacob Lipschitz, Rabbi Elhanan's secretary, to negotiate with the young baron in a peaceful manner. "This is a golden rule," Rabbi Salanter said. "One must begin to negotiate with peaceful words."[11] He recommended caution and diplomacy. Rabbi Elhanan had just become acquainted with the baron, and it was therefore not advisable to do anything that would cause a breach in their relationship.

Rabbi Elhanan decided to send a letter of protest to the baron and a copy of it to Rabbi Salanter, who was concerned about the tone and wording of the letter and its possible result. On October 13, 1882, Rabbi Lipschitz received a letter from Rabbi Salanter, urging him to use all means at his disposal to pressure the young baron to give up his idea of reopening the seminary.[12]

Some weeks later the results of the negotiations were still not known. Rabbi Salanter wrote another letter to Rabbi Lipschitz, in which he referred to talks he had had with the young baron in Paris.[13] Rabbi Lipschitz published five letters sent him by Rabbi Salanter in the last weeks of his life.[14] All dealt with Rabbi Salanter's concern about the Vilna seminary and about the preservation of traditional Judaism. In the very last letter he wrote:

> . . . although the project to reestablish the rabbinical seminary was abolished, yet the decree that the rabbis must pass the requirements of studies that are in a country school is still in force. Therefore, one must beware lest the

---

[10]Jacob Lipschitz, *Sichron Jacob* (Kovna, 1930), III, 125.

[11]*Ibid.*, p. 126f. Reference to Deuteronomy 20:10, "When thou drawest nigh unto a city to fight against it, then proclaim peace unto it. . . ."

[12]See letter from Rabbi Salanter to Rabbi Lipschitz, October 13, 1882, in *Sichron Jacob*, III, p. 131.

[13]See letter from Rabbi Salanter to Rabbi Lipschitz, December 4, 1882, in *Sichron Jacob*, III, p. 131.

[14]*Ibid.*, p. 131f.

barons[15] see their hopes realized. The fundamental fault here is that because of this requirement, God forbid, the study of rabbinics may decline, decisions for instructions may be lessened . . . as has been the case in Germany. With the Orthodox, it is more important that the candidates know the Code of Laws and be God-fearing. Those who are versed in the matter of learning and instructing, which as yet is what we know—since knowledge, thank God, has not been extinguished—realize that erudition is necessary to be able to render decisions. According to current tendencies one cannot know if there be found such scholars in Torah. . . .[16]

Rabbi Salanter from the very start opposed the rabbinical seminaries of Vilna and Zhitomir. He was forced to leave Russia because of them and before his death on February 3, 1883, he witnessed the failure of Baron David Gunzburg's proposition.

The Attitude toward Dr. Max Lilienthal's School Reforms

Rabbi Salanter understood the motives of the Russian government behind the school reforms in the Jewish Pale of Settlement.[17] Nicholas I wanted to make changes in traditional Judaism along the lines of Reform Judaism in Germany. Therefore Dr. Max Lilienthal (1815-1882), a German Jew, was assigned to carry out Nicholas' scheme. In February, 1841, Lilienthal was called to St. Petersburg. He tried to persuade Minister of Education Uvarov to abolish all private schools and to halt instruction by all private teachers. Lilienthal wanted to import an entire staff of teachers from Germany. In his memoirs, he writes that he mentioned to the Minister of Education that all obstacles in the path of the desired reeduca-

---

[15]This refers to the Gunzburgs.

[16]Letter from Rabbi Salanter to Rabbi Lipschitz, January 7, 1883, in *Sichron Jacob*, III, 132 and in M. G. Glenn, *Israel Salanter, op. cit.*, p. 105f.

[17]Pale of Jewish Settlement refers to certain restricted districts of Tsarist Russia in which Jews were given the right to live in 1792. The statute of 1835 "defined more definitely" the Pale of Settlement which was to include the provinces of Vilna, Grodno, Volhynia, Minsk, Bessarabia, Podolia, Bialystok, Ekaterinoslav, Kiev (except the city of Kiev), Kherson (without Nikolaev), Moghilev and Vitebsk (without the villages), Taurida (without Sevastopol), Chernigov and Poltova (without the Cossack villages). In addition, Courland, Latvia, and the provinces of the Kingdom of Poland with were later annexed by Russia in 1863, were added to the Pale. The boundaries set by the decree of 1855 remained more or less intact until 1917. Salo Baron, *The Russian Jew* (New York, 1964), p. 39.

tion of the Jews in Russia would vanish, were the Tsar to give the Jews complete emancipation. To this the Minister of Education replied that the initial "push" must come from the Jews themselves, in order to "deserve the favor of the Sovereign." Lilienthal accepted the task of touring the Jewish Pale of Settlement, of organizing there the few in favor of the Enlightenment, and of spreading the plan of school reform among the Orthodox Jewish masses.[18]

Lilienthal pondered the inconsistency of the government. He could not comprehend why Nicholas I exerted himself to reeducate the Jews when the Jews were on a higher cultural level than the masses of Russians.[19] Since the Tsar distrusted education in general, his attempt to educate the Jews could lead only to suspicion. S. M. Solovev writes that with the crowning of Nicholas I, education ceased to be a virtue and came to be regarded as a crime.[20] The Tsar's concern with the education of the Jewish people in Russia caused a Russian educator to remark: "In the matter of education, Jews, who were regarded as a harmful element of the population, were put in an unusually privileged position as compared with the tens of millions of the Russian population who were not regarded as harmful."[21]

Lilienthal came to Vilna in the beginning of 1842, and promptly called a gathering of the Jewish community. He explained the plan formulated by the government and by Uvarov, "the friend of the Jews." He was heard with suspicion, as he tells us in his memoirs:

> The elders sat there absorbed in deep contemplation. Some of them, leaning on their silver-adorned staffs or smoothing their long beards, seemed as if agitated by earnest thoughts and justifiable suspicions; others were engaging in a lively but quiet discussion on the principles involved; such put to me the ominous question: "Doctor, are you fully acquainted with the leading principles of our government? You are a stranger; do you know what you are undertaking? The course pursued against all denominations but the Greek proves clearly that the Government intends

---

[18]*Ibid.*, p. 53.
[19]David Philipson, *Max Lilienthal* (New York, 1915), p. 19.
[20]S. M. Solovev, *Zapiski*, p. 120.
[21]A. Beletsky, *Vepres Ob Obraz. Russ. Ev. V. Tsarst. Imp. Nicol. Per.*, p. 40.

to have but one church in the whole Empire; that it has in view only its own future strength and greatness and not our future prosperity. We are sorry to state that we put no confidence in the new measures proposed by the ministerial council, and that we look with gloomy foreboding into the future."[22]

Lilienthal warned the elders of Vilna that their unwillingness to cooperate would not stop the government from carrying out its plans. On the other hand, if they were willing to support the project, their recommendations would be taken into account in formulating the policies of the Jewish school system. At this point, the elders' resistance weakened, but still they wanted a guarantee that their religious practice would not be curtailed. Lilienthal promised the Jews of Vilna that as soon as he "discovered that any measures against our holy religion were being undertaken, he would resign from his office."[23] His promise enabled the elders of Vilna to give the program their support.

From Vilna Lilienthal went to Minsk, where he met stiff opposition. Traditional Jews countered his arguments with the following attack:

As long as we are not granted civil rights, education will be only a misfortune for us. In his present cultural state the Jew does not disdain the humiliating livelihood of a broker or usurer, and finds comfort in religion. But when the Jew receives a modern education, he will become sensitive to his legal sensibilities, and then, dissatisfied with his bitter lot, he will be prompted to desert his faith. An honest Jewish father will never agree to train his child for conversion.[24]

Lilienthal had more success in the southwest. In the cities of Berdichev and Odessa, he was greeted royally. Here the Jews were inspired by the ideas of the Enlightenment. Lilienthal outlined the plans of the Russian government at a gathering of representative Jews, and they pledged full cooperation

---

[22]David Philipson, *op. cit.*, p. 264.
[23]Louis Greenberg, *The Jews in Russia* (New Haven, 1965), I, p. 35.
[24]*Ibid.*, p. 35f.

The followers of the Enlightenment were the staunchest supporters of the establishment of Jewish government-sponsored schools. The Russian-Jewish followers of the Enlightenment hailed Nicholas and Uvarov in verse and prose. A prayer of thanksgiving, composed by Vilna historian Samuel Joseph Fuenn (1819-1891), is typical of the praise and naive exaltation the Tsar's undertaking evoked from lovers of the Enlightenment. Fuenn gave thanks to God, Who caused the Jewish people to be favorable and graceful in the eyes of the exalted rulers of Russia; the heart of Nicholas I, said Fuenn, was full of pure love for his Jewish subjects. According to Fuenn the Tsar's throne was the seat of justice and righteousness.[25]

From abroad, too, men of the Enlightenment raised their voices in praise of Nicholas I and Uvarov. Abraham Goldberg of Rava, Galicia, wrote a poem entitled "Masa Zafon" ("A Prophecy from the North"). In the poem he takes his brethren to task for their lack of appreciation of the blessings of education and agriculture. He depicts Nicholas, moved by compassion, saying to himself, "I shall be like dew to the children of Israel, I shall be a source of living waters to him."[26]

The disciples of the Enlightenment in Russia and in Western Europe were unsuccessful in their attempts to change the attitude of the masses of Russian Jewry. The reaction of most Russian Jews to government Jewish education is well told by the novelist Lev Levanda, in his short story *Shkoloboiazn* (*School Fear*). It appears, from the tale, that school reform was thought of as an evil decree, similar to military service.

On November 13, 1884, Nicholas I approved two enactments, one a public decree calling for the education of the Jewish youth, the other a secret rescript (official decree) dispatched to the Minister of Public Instruction. The public enactment ordered the setting up of Jewish schools of two grades, and of two rabbinical seminaries for the training of rabbis and teachers. The teachers of the Jewish government-sponsored schools were to be both Jews and Christians. The graduates of these schools were given a reduction in the term of military obligation. The responsibility for the es-

---

[25]S. M. Fuenn, *Pirhe Zafon*, II, 70-72.
[26]A. Goldberg, "Masa Zafon," p. 21.

tablishment of the schools in the respective localities was granted to school boards, composed of Jews and Christians.

In the confidential rescript the orders were entirely different. The purpose of the training of the Jews was to bring them closer to the Christian population and to eradicate the prejudices resulting from the study of the Talmud. With the opening of the new Jewish schools the old ones were to be gradually closed or reorganized. As soon as the Crown schools were established in sufficient numbers, attendance at them would become obligatory. The superintendents of the new schools were to be chosen only from among Christians. Every possible effort was to be made to put obstacles in the way of granting licenses to the melammeds (teachers) who lacked a secular education. Finally, after the passing of twenty years, no one was to be eligible to be a teacher or a rabbi unless he had obtained his degree from one of the government rabbinical seminaries.[27]

It was not long, however, before the secret came out. The Jews of Russia were grieved at the idea of being stripped of their educational independence, and decided on passive resistance to all government degrees. School reform progressed slowly.

Lilienthal Departs in Defeat

Max Lilienthal, not unaware of the purpose of the Jewish government-sponsored schools and the seminaries in Vilna and Zhitomir, suddenly abandoned his post at the Ministry of Public Instruction in 1845, and left Russia forever.

Before leaving for America, Lilienthal stated that the only way for the Jews to make peace with Nicholas I was "[to bow down] before the Greek cross."[28] He had finally come to the conclusion that the Tsar's policy was "to assign a plausible reason for every act done by the Government in order to stand justified in the eyes of the world, especially in Western Europe."[29]

In the United States, Lilienthal held important pulpits in New York and Cincinnati. He died in Cincinnati in 1882.

---

[27] S. M. Dubnow, *op. cit.,* p. 58.

[28] *Ibid.,* p. 59.

[29] Jacob S. Raisin, *The Haskalah Movement in Russia* (Philadelphia, 1913), p. 179.

Two Men, Two Viewpoints

"Who is wise?—He who foresees results."[30]

Rabbi Israel Salanter was endowed with clear vision and true foresight. He was able to foresee the consequences of pseudo-Haskalah in the days of Max Lilienthal. He was able to see through the scheme of Tsar Nicholas' school reforms.

At about the time Rabbi Salanter began his activities on behalf of Torah Judaism, Lilienthal also assumed his responsibilities. The former was from a town where Orthodox Judaism flourished. The later came from a city where Jews were under the influence of modern culture.

Rabbi Salanter personified Orthodox Judaism, Lilienthal—the German Haskalah. Rabbi Salanter was the prototype of the true rabbi, the type detested by the Maskilim, while Lilienthal typified the modern, cultured gentleman.

The two also differed in their concept of Jewishness. Rabbi Salanter, a product of his environment, was an Eastern European Jew in word and manner. Lilienthal clung to his fellow Jews, yet at the same time he despised the very speech of his people.[31] He disapproved of their habits and looked away from them toward the world of the Enlightenment. Rabbi Salanter advised his fellow Jews to "know themselves." He told them that if enlightenment was to come, it had to come from within. Lilienthal, on the other hand, felt that the Russian Jews must "know the world." Salvation, in his opinion, would come to them only from the outside.

It seemed at first that Max Lilienthal would emerge as master of the situation. However, as it turned out, it took only a few years for Rabbi Salanter to be vindicated, and Lilienthal's work ended in a fiasco.[32]

Attitude toward the Verbal Attacks by the Maskilim

Many of the great Hebrew writers of the day were guilty of gossip, slander, and ridicule against the rabbis. They used these means to advance the ideals of Haskalah. Abraham Mapu's (1808-

---

[30]See *Avoth*, II, 13.

[31]See David Philipson, *Max Lilienthal, op. cit.*, pp. 22-45. See also M. G. Glenn, *Israel Salanter, op. cit.*, p. 39.

[32]See S. Rosenfeld, *Rabbi Israel Salanter* (Warsaw, 1911), p. 7. See also M. G. Glenn, *op. cit.*, p. 39.

1867) [33] realistic novel *Ayit Zavua* (*The Painted Hawk*) depicts a certain rabbi under the name of Rabbi Gadiel as a blind fanatic, an enemy of Haskalah and Hebrew literature. Mapu portrayed him in the darkest colors as the mortal enemy of culture.[34] He accused the rabbis of hypocrisy and said that fanatical spiritual leaders were persecuting the champions of the Enlightenment. Mapu even sacrificed truth on the altar of his belief: all that was Haskalah was very good, noble, and just; everything opposed to it was fanatic, hypocritical, cowardly, and wicked. This novel presented an exaggerated description of Jewish life in Kovna at the time in which both Rabbi Salanter and Mapu lived there.

Likewise, the poet Judah Leib Gordon (1830-1892),[35] in his "Kotzo shel Yod" ("Dot over I"),[36] attacked the strictness of the rabbis, but in doing so he degraded Jewish law. Whlie attacking the strictness of the rabbis of his age, in doing so he maligned the Shulhan Arukh (Jewish Code of Law) as well. He also did not distinguish between strict rabbis and compassionate ones. Gordon wrote the following:

> Our people live on air; the new generation is brought up in the Heder [Hebrew school] under dogmatic and ignorant teachers; Rabbis busy themselves with hairsplitting studies that are absolutely worthless, and pay no regard whatever to the needs of the people. Shall such conditions remain as they are: Do they need no improvement? . . . We must not stand by idle. It is the duty of everyone who has the interests of his people at heart to fight against such conditions. All the fences around the law might have been necessary at the time they were instituted, but they are superfluous today. I do not believe in destroying all memories of the past with which the life of our people is bound up, or in giving up hope of a future. . . . I seek the golden

---

[33]See Joseph Klausner, *Historia Shel ha-Sifruth ha-Hadasah* (Jerusalem, 1954), I, pp. 323-352.

[34]See Abraham Mapu, *Ayit Zavua* (Tel. Aviv, 1909), p. 225. See also M. G. Glenn, *Rabbi Israel Salanter*, *op. cit.*, p. 43. Glenn identifies Rabbi Gadiel as Rabbi Salanter, who was the personification of truth and morality.

[35]See Joseph Klausner, *op. cit.*, II, pp. 94-136.

[36]Yod is the smallest letter in the Hebrew alphabet. The poem in question pictures the tragedy of a woman who remained unhappy the rest of her life because the Hebrew bill of divorce which she had obtained from her husband was declared void on account of a trifling error in spelling.

mean: to unite pure faith with reason and the needs of
the time. Only by an orderly system of education combining secular knowledge with Judaism and the love of our
people can we prepare ourselves for better days.[37]

Faith not based on understanding is worse than atheism. Every day you reiterate your belief in the coming of
the Messiah; but you that await his miraculous arrival
daily, and the German reformers that disregard the prayer
for his advent, alike deny the great principle. Miracles do
not happen every day. The recital of the prayer is merely
mechanical; you don't think of what you say. Suppose the
Messiah does come; what good can he expect from you?
From among the educated Jews he can appoint his officers, physicians, secretaries, etc. But what can you accomplish with your pilpulistic [hairsplitting] arguments, and
the study of the Maharshah? Will you become the law-
givers, and reestablish the "four corporal" and other pun-
ishments, for the least violation of the most insignificant
practices? Will not other nations rise against you and destroy you in one day?[38]

Judah Gordon held that the rabbis must prepare the younger
generation for the coming of the Messiah in a natural way, namely
by giving the intelligent that useful education in secular knowledge which a modern man must possess.[39] Those who are not capable of study must learn trades and occupations. Merchants must
be taught by the rabbis to be scrupulously honest in their dealings
with both Jews and non-Jews. The rabbis must institute order in
the conduct of communal affairs; and they must eradicate from the
hearts of the young the prejudice toward other religions and their
adherents.[40] The rabbis must realize that the time has come to make
changes by encouraging the young in the hederim and yeshivoth to
follow the enlightened ideas of the Haskalah and to enjoy its

---

[37]See Judah Gordon, *Iggerot*, edited by Isaac Jacob Weisberg (Warsaw, Suldberg Bros., 1894), I, p. 148. See also Abraham Benedict Rhine, *Leon Gordon* (Philadelphia, Jewish Publication Society), p. 53.

[38]See Judah Gordon, *Iggerot*, *op. cit.*, I, pp. 172-173. See also Abraham Benedict Rhine, *Leon Gordon*, *op. cit.*, p. 54.

[39]See Judah Gordon, "Bimah le-Toeh Ruah" in *Iggerot*, *op. cit.*, I, p. 173.

[40]*Ibid.*

fruits.[41] The rabbis must face reality and institute reforms to meet the challenges of the day. They must stop bickering about the qualifications of the ritual slaughterers and devote more time to solving the educational problems of the young who are taught by "slaughtering teachers."[42] Is it not more important to develop new methods of teaching than to waste precious time determining whether this one or that one is qualified to slaughter the cow or the fowl in accordance with Rabbinic law?[43] From childhood until marriage, the young are permitted only the study of Talmud. How can the rabbis allow Jewish daughters to grow up illiterate, and how can they expect them to become capable mothers when they themselves have not been properly educated during their childhood?[44]

Judah Gordon's attitude toward the rabbis was one of bitter antagonism. He could never forgive them for their indifference toward the needs of the time and their refusal of reform. He blamed the rabbis for all the misfortunes of the Jews and for their ignorance of the ways of the world. In the heat of his war upon ignorance, Judah Gordon used sarcasm unsparingly against the rabbis and Talmudic teachers, the latter the product of the former. Thus, for example, in his satire "Barburim Abusim," Judah Gordon ridicules the tendencies of the rabbis to interpret the ritual laws in the strictest sense. A poor woman bought two turkeys in the winter, and pampered them up to the time of Pesah (Passover), and thought with delight of the festive times she and her large family would have during the festival week; how she would sell a portion of the meat to her rich neighbor, and with the proceeds buy matzoth and wine for her family, and how she would use the unsold part for her children. The turkeys were slaughtered accordingly on Pesah eve. Unfortunately, a red spot was detected on the esophagus of each bird. Frightened, the woman ran to the rabbi. Although there was no blood or any perforation, the rabbi declared them prohibited for use, because the esophagus may have been perforated and may have healed. The poor woman remained without food for the holiday. Gordon comforts her in her adversity, caused by the mercilessness of the rabbis, with the following words: "You must not despair,

---

[41]*Ibid.*
[42]See Judah Gordon, "Binah le-Toeh Ruah" in *Ha-Meliz* No. 40, 1870, p. 305.
[43]*Ibid.*
[44]*Ibid.*

poor woman. Jews are charitable; you can support yourself by begging."[45]

In his novelette *Kaf Regel Egel*[46] Gordon tells of a rabbi who, on a certain Sabbath morning, declared all the meat unkosher at the instigation of his wife, who was angered because she had not succeeded in getting the portion of veal she liked. The poet's charges of partiality in judgment, and the interpretation of the law for selfish ends, are unjust. The rabbis were scrupulous men. Gordon is likewise unfair in blaming the rabbis for the misfortunes of the Jews.

The rabbis themselves were the product of the historical forces that have made Judaism what it is. Therefore, they were the result rather than the cause of Jewish isolation. The question may be asked: what would have become of Judaism, during so many ages of persecution, had the rabbis been more yielding and removed the fences around the law? With the least breath of freedom, many Jews were prepared to abandon the restrictions Judaism imposed upon them and become traitors to their brethren. The poet Judah Gordon himself acknowledged it; therefore how could the rabbis themselves have sanctioned such action? Gordon wrote in an undated letter that the complaints of the ultra-Orthodox against the Haskalah and the Maskilim were not without grounds, though not for the reasons assigned by them. "To our sorrow we must realize that the culture we are striving after will make us drink gall, and produce thistles instead of flowers."[47] Gordon laments not because of the customs neglected, or the fences broken down, or the burden of practices and observances thrown off; but because the unruly waters have reached to the very soul of our religion; and a sharp sword lies at the very throat of our faith and its existence.[48] A true Haskalah, like that of Saadia, Maimonides, and Mendelssohn, is very rare among us; an imaginary destructive Haskalah prevails.[49] "The Maskilim have taken the shell of civilization and dressed themselves in it for appearance's sake; but the kernel they have thrown away. They are not particular about religious precepts, and have no scruples about adopting even the practices that have given

---

[45]See Judah Gordon, *Kol Shirei*, IV, Satire 9.
[46]See Judah Gordon, *Kol Kitbe*, I.
[47]See Judah Gordon, *Iggerot, op. cit.*, I, p. 438.
[48]*Ibid.*
[49]*Ibid.*

Israel his unenviable reputation among the Gentiles. The Maskilim of the better sort are truly educated men, but they are traitors, and they are ashamed of their race."[50]

In light of the above views, it appears that the rabbis were justified in opposing a movement that tended to produce such a progeny. Gordon, however, had a theory of his own, founded on an historical basis, with regard to the tendency to go to extremes. He wrote:

> The struggle between the old and the new that is going on in our midst now is the result of a natural development. A person accustomed to a certain line of conduct, or given to one extreme, who desires to habituate himself to the mean, goes first to the opposite extreme, until the two extremes are united, and he returns to the golden mean. The tendency of the present generation toward the extreme of modern civilization is a natural result of the former tendency toward the extreme of religiousness, and there is hope that in the end the extremists will return and meet on common ground. Our religion even in its first, its Mosaic, form did not strike root in the hearts of our people in one generation. "The Book and the Sword were always wrapped together." Many generations and centuries passed, and not without wars and confusion, before Israel removed the strange gods from his midst. Many generations and centuries passed also after that, not without schisms and dissensions, until the Mosaic became the Jewish religion, and until the Rabbinic law spread and became an integral part of Judaism. We who were born many ages after these struggles and revolutions, and who try to lead a peaceful life, are disturbed when we see that the age of excommunication has returned, and the struggle has been renewed. The days of disorder may be prolonged; but the spirit of God which has been with us ever since the beginning of our history will finally produce a substance solid and perfect out of those mixed elements. The useless ingredients will disappear, and the solid and living matter will survive, and form the foundation of the new, improved world."[51]

---

[50]*Ibid.*
[51]*Ibid.*, II, 439. See also Abraham Rhine, *Leon Gordon, op. cit.*, p. 60f.

Thus, according to Judah Gordon, in order to bring about the "golden mean" it became necessary to combat ignorance and superstition, to remove, as it were, the weeds that had grown over the vineyard of the Lord—and which the rabbis guarded as carefully as though they formed part and parcel of the vineyard. Therefore, Gordon fought the rabbis. Then when the opposite tendency manifested itself he battled the Maskilim, in order to pave the way for the golden mean.

A contemporary of Judah Gordon, Moses Leib Lilienblum (1843-1910),[52] also held that the dominant rabbinism in its medievalism did not represent the true essence of Judaism. Lilienblum's interpretation of reform called not for a revolution but for an evolution of Judaism. Just as the Talmud had once reformed Judaism in accordance with the teachings of its time, so must Judaism be reformed by us, said Lilienblum, in accordance with the demands of our time.[53]

Lilienblum felt that the rabbis did not realize that they erred when they issued decrees derived from minutiae.[54] He wanted rabbinic law changed to alleviate the hardships of the Jews in their adjustment to the era of progress and enlightenment.[55]

When the youthful Lilienblum published these views in a series of articles in the *Ha-Meliz* under the title "Orhot ha-Talmud" ("The Ways of the Talmud") the Orthodox townsmen were so incensed that it was unsafe for him to stay in his home town of Vilkomir.

His views on reforms in Judaism having been deemed unacceptable by the rabbis, Lilienblum proceeded to write an even harsher series of articles, this time attacking the rabbis and the Shulhan Arukh. He criticized the rabbis for "sitting with folded hands" and failing to remove the burdensome teachings of the Talmud.[56] He believed that the laws of the Talmud and the Shulhan Arukh *must* be changed to conform with the times.[57] He denied the sacredness of these laws. He asked the rabbis: "How can you

---

[52]See Joseph Klausner, *op. cit.*, II, 64-93.
[53]See Moses Leib Lilienblum, "Orhot ha-Talmud" in *Kol Kitbe Moses Leib Lilienblum* (Cracow, Joseph Fisher Publishers, 1910), p. 30f.
[54]*Ibid.*, 36f.
[55]*Ibid.*
[56]*Ibid.*, p. 51.
[57]*Ibid.*, pp. 49-51.

prove that all the decrees of the Talmud and the laws of the Shul-han Arukh cannot be changed in accordance with the times? How can you prove that a Beth Din (a rabbinical court) in our times cannot void the decisions of former generations? . . . Who taught you that the decrees of one man or many men, even if they are the greatest of their time, have to have the authority to prohibit a thing for eternity?"[58]

Moses Lilienblum was compelled to leave Vilkomir for Odessa. There, in 1870, Lilienblum wrote his rhymed satire *Kohal Refa'im* (*The Congregation of the Dead*), in which the dark shadows of a Jewish town—the elders, the rabbis, and other righteous and worthy men—move weirdly about the gloom of the nether world.

Rabbi Blazer is Attacked

The poet Judah Leib Gordon attacked verbally one of the most outstanding disciples of Rabbi Israel Salanter and the Musar Movement, Rabbi Isaac Blazer (1837-1907).[59] Rabbi Blazer bemoaned the low moral climate of his day in the following manner: "Piety has declined immensely . . . houses of worship are deserted, sins have multiplied beyond control, ugly traits mount . . . falsehood will replace righteousness, and truth is lacking."[60] In 1862 Rabbi Blazer was advised by Rabbi Salanter to accept the rabbinate in St. Petersburg.

St. Petersburg was the center for the Enlightenment in Russia. Judah Gordon came to St. Petersburg as secretary of the Society for the Diffusion of the Enlightenment. The new Hebrew periodical *Ha-Shahar* (*The Morning*) published some of his contemporary epics, in which he poured forth his anger against Rabbinism. He portrays the misfortune of a Jewish woman forced to marry at the bidding of the marriage broker, without experiencing love and happiness. The poet decries the Orthodox leaders of the community, who betray the young pioneers of the Enlightenment to the Russian police. He objected to the prevalence of the spiritual over the secular in the whole evolution of Judaism. He berated even the great prophet Jeremiah, who in besieged Jerusalem advocated sub-

---

[58]See Moses Lieb Lilienblum, "Al Davar Ha-Tikunim B'Dat" in *Kol Kitbe Moses Lieb Lilienblum*, *op. cit.*, p. 115.
[59]See Benjamin Katznelson, "Kol Yaakov" in *Ha-Tzfira*, No. 18, 1890.
[60]See Isaac Blazer, *Or Israel*, *op. cit.*, p. 4.

mission to the Babylonians and strict observance of the law. The prophet, a symbol of the contemporary rabbi, was depicted by Gordon as "law above life."[61] The implication was clear: Jewish life must be secularized.

In St. Petersburg, Gordon saw the sore spots in the new enlightened generation of Jews. Educated Jews were abandoning Jewish ways and the Hebrew tongue. He wrote in anguish: "For whom do I labor?" He felt that the youth, estranged from the foundation of Jewish culture, would no more be able to understand the "Songs of Zion."

The Maskil Nahum Adadawski accused Rabbi Blazer of educating outstanding young Talmudists in the spirit of asceticism and alienation from Jewish communal life. He wrote: "He is unfit to educate rabbis in the spirit of Rabbi Israel Salanter because of his fanaticism. . . ."[62] Adadawski held Rabbi Blazer responsible for causing the madness of some of the ascetic musar students as well as for the maladjustment of others to Jewish society.[63]

Rabbi Blazer did not remain aloof. He attacked the Maskilim and the assimilationists vigorously. He fought for the necessity of preserving traditional Judaism and reinforcing it with morality and ethics. He confronted the insults of the Maskilim and accepted them as a reason for continuing to wage war against the violators of traditional Judaism and musar.[64]

Although men like Gordon and Adadawski attacked Rabbi Blazer, other men of the Enlightenment recognized the spiritual strength and truthfulness in Rabbi Blazer's personality and they became his admirers.[65]

One of these, Benjamin Katznelson, wrote that he heard the abuse and mockery that the poet Judah Leib Gordon had heaped upon Rabbi Blazer; but when he had the opportunity to meet the rabbi in St. Peterburg in person, his character, his good deeds, and

[61]See Gordon's poem, "Tzidkiyyahu be-bet ha-pekuddot" ("Zedekiah in Prison"), in which the defeated and blinded Judean ruler (See Jeremiah 52:11) bitterly complains of the evil effects of the prophetic doctrine.

[62]See Nahum Adadawski, "Esh Yatzah Me'Hesbon" in Ha-Meliz, No. 22, January 26, 1890, 1-2.

[63]Ibid.

[64]See Isaac Blazer, "Elbonah shel Torah" in Ha-Tzfira, 18, 1890. See also Isaac Blazer, Or Israel, op. cit., p. 4. See also Dov Katz, Tenuah ha-Musar, op. cit., II, p. 224.

[65]See Benjamin Katznelson, "Kol Yaakov" in Ha-Tzfira, 81, 1900.

his determination surpassed those of Judah Leib Gordon and of his other detractors.[66] Katznelson held that "even though one can find fault with the rabbis and the followers of musar for their opposition to Zionism and their narrow-minded outlook on life, they are innocent since they were nurtured since childhood by their parents and teachers to acquire such attitudes. However, the Maskilim, cosmopolitan in their outlook, must know better than to attack verbally sincere and dedicated spiritual leaders."[67]

The eminent poet Hillel Babli wrote a poem of adoration for Rabbi Blazer, describing him in the following manner: "He was the moving spirit of the musar sect and the true mantle-bearer of Rabbi Israel Salanter. Righteousness, wisdom, decisiveness, and charisma are his attributes. . . ."[68]

There is little doubt from primary source material that Rabbi Isaac Blazer was a man of integrity and determination. He was convinced, as was his teacher, Rabbi Salanter, that traditional Judaism revitalized by musar and imbued with ethical practice would preserve the Jewish heritage. Gordon and the Maskilim were willing to make changes in the traditional Jewish rituals in order to adjust the Jew to modern living. However, they failed to realize that reform within traditional Judaism was not a guarantee of alleviating the social, political, cultural, and economic discriminations against the Jews in Tsarist Russia. Gordon saw the purpose of Tsar Nicholas' project of enlightening the Jews through secular education and modern rabbinical seminaries. At the same time, Maskilim like Katnelson, and others, took notice of the Mussar Movement, and lauded the goals of its followers.

Rabbi Zissel's Attitude

Rabbi Simhah Zissel of Kelm, one of Rabbi Salanter's confidants, was influenced to some extent by secular education.[69] He appreciated the practical need for secular subjects.[70] He decided to combine Torah and some secular subjects in his school curriculum.[71] Even though he did not emulate the aspirations of the true Mas-

---

[66]*Ibid.*

[67]*Ibid.*

[68]See Hillel Babli, "Rav Itzele Bayaarah" in *Bitzaron*, 6, 1928, 44-49.

[69]See Eliezer E. Friedman, *Sefer Ha-Zichromoth 1858-1926* (Tel Aviv, 1926), p. 81.

[70]*Ibid.*

[71]*Ibid.*

kilim of his time in introducing the whole gamut of Haskalah in his school, still, in accordance with his understanding and taste, he succeeded in coordinating the teachings of the Torah with carefully selected teachings of the secular subjects.[72]

There is no record of verbal attack on Rabbi Zissel by the Maskilim. This is because he did not manifest an openly hostile attitude toward the Haskalah movement, but rather displayed an attitude of tolerance and readiness to adopt some of its ideas. He was also by nature a true lover of mankind, attempting to avoid those situations which engender gossip and talebearing. It may be said that he actually had more difficulty with the rabbis who opposed the Musar Movement and his schools in Kelm and Grobin than he had from the followers of the Enlightenment.

Rabbi Joshua Heller.

Among the loyal students of Rabbi Salanter was Rabbi Joshua Heller (1814-1880). He was considered an outstanding Torah authority of his generation. His views on the Enlightenment are unique because he blamed the rudiments of Torah study as the main factor in the laxity of observance and faith in God. He did not agree with other rabbis that the ideas of the Enlightenment were responsible for leading many young people away from traditional Judaism. He wrote that the study of languages, history, geography, and mathematics should not be prohibited; after all, other educational skills were not prohibited and they were not conducive to the breaking up of religious practice. In the past, he felt, secular learning and religious observance went hand in hand without causing heresy among the young.[73]

Rabbi Heller attributed the heresy in the young to mechanical learning in childhood. He believed that teachers failed to indoctrinate young people with the fundamentals of religious faith; thus, a youth exposed to contradictions lacked the basic principles of faith to withstand conflict.[74]

According to Rabbi Heller the Haskalah could be useful, provided a person was equipped from childhood with the basic practices of Judaism. In essence, he felt, the environment of the En-

---

[72]Ibid.
[73]See Joshua Heller, *Maoz Ha-Dat* (Jerusalem, 1903), chapter 10.
[74]Ibid.

lightenment presented no dilemma to the sincere religious believer. He berated parents for setting a bad example to their children in providing only a mechanical application of the religious laws.

A Lesson for the Present

Rabbi Heller's views—strong religious convictions and meaningful observance at home, taught from childhood—have a certain meaning for the youth who presently invade our colleges, ill prepared to defend Judaism, Israel and morality in a culture characterized by the breakdown of the family unit and laxity of morals. Even yeshiva students are prey to the evils of our time, because they come to college without strong convictions and with a naive and sheltered idea of Judaism. The views of Rabbi Heller are timely and relevant.

Rabbi Joseph Yozel Hurwitz

Rabbi Joseph Yozel Hurwitz was criticized for his eccentric behavior which provided the opponents of the Musar Movement with an excuse for blaming it for the unusual conduct of the man. As a student in the Kovna musar seminary he witnessed the death of his wife in childbirth. This misfortune depressed him to such an extent that he decided to isolate himself from the world.[75] He lived in the house of Shlomo Hapech of Slobodca. However, he stayed in a room and locked himself up for a year and nine months (during 1882-1883). Food was delivered through small windows by ringing a bell and placing a note for the necessities on the window. The philanthropist Obediah Lachman provided the necessary funds to support him and to construct a ritual bath.

During the isolation in his room, Rabbi Hurwitz did not go to synagogue on the Sabbath and holidays, and did not even permit himself to hear the blowing of the horn on the New Year. Most of the time he studied law and musar. From time to time his voice was heard when he passed judgment on himself by shouting, "Lord of the Universe, I have to humble myself," or "We have to arrive already at the point of using common sense and sound judgment."[76] It appears that he worked very hard to strengthen his faith.[77]

---

[75]See Y. L. Nekritz, "Yeshivath Navaradock" (Nek York, 1956), p. 248.
[76]Told by Rabbi Zelig Tarsis, a contemporary of Rabbi Hurwitz in Dov Katz, *Tenuath ha-Musar, op. cit.,* IV, p. 188.
[77]See Y. L. Nekritz, *op. cit.,* p. 248.

The incident of his isolation gave the followers of the Enlightenment and the dissenters to the Musar Movement a weapon with
which to criticize and to mock the teachings of the Musar Movement.[78] The Maskilim began to write articles about the eccentricity
of Rabbi Hurwitz, and used the isolation incident to ridicule the
Musar Movement and musar.[79] Also, outstanding rabbis like Rabbi
Isaac Elhanan felt that it could lead to desecration of God's name.
He urged Rabbi Hurwitz to come out. Rabbi Simhah Zissel, on the
other hand, did not see any desecration of God's name if a person
"locks himself up to dedicate himself to Torah and God-fearing."[80]
Rabbi Blazer tried to persuade him to come out of seclusion. Rabbi
Elhanan sent his sexton to urge the exodus, but without results.
Rabbi Elhanan, speaking through the sexton, asked Rabbi Hurwitz
why he did not go to the synagogue to hear the blowing of the horn
on the New Year. Rabbi Hurwitz answered:

> Why is there a law of preference in the case of abstaining
> from evil or doing good? Surely, to abstain from doing evil
> is the preferred one. Thus, it is more important to remove
> oneself from people and to save oneself from hatred, jeal-
> ousy, passion . . . than to hear the blowing of the horn
> in an unethical environment.[81]

When Rabbi Elhanan told him that it was possible to do both, to
live among people and to keep the laws according to the Shulhan
Arukh, and at the same time to renounce the evil emotions of
hatred, jealousy, and passion, Rabbi Hurwitz answered that he had
not yet reached such a standard.[82]

When the Tsarist government learned of Rabbi Hurwitz's isolation, it interpreted it as indicating that he was preoccupied with
revolutionary activities, and thus forced him to come out in the
open.[83]

The Maskilim criticized Rabbi Hurwitz for his asceticism, eccentric behavior, and isolation from the community. They felt that

---

[78]Ibid.
[79]See Moses Joshua Levin, "Nazirei Israel" in Ha-Meliz, 18, 1883, pp. 276-277.
[80]Told by Rabbi Dov Dessler in the name of Simhah Zissel, content in Dov
Katz, Tenuath ha-Musar, op. cit., IV, p. 188.
[81]Ibid.
[82]Ibid.
[83]See Moses Joshua Levin, "Nazirei Israel," op. cit. See also I. L. Nekritz, "Yeshivath Navaradock," op. cit., p. 248.

he and others, who isolated themselves from society, were not productive in solving the economic, educational, and political problems of the Jews. They looked upon these people as exploiters of other Jews. The Maskilim did not object to musar but to the effects of musar, especially if men were influenced toward isolation rather than to communal participation, to self-spiritual, educational, and moral betterment rather than to the improvement of these qualities in others.

Although Rabbi Hurwitz, in his youth as well as in his later years, tried to avoid controversy with the Maskilim, nevertheless he expressed his views on the Haskalah and the Maskilim as follows:

"The cursed Haskalah led astray many and defiled the hearts of the people. It caused many to hate the word of God and it split the outside world with the world of yeshivoth."[84]

There is no doubt from the above passage that Rabbi Hurwitz found the Haskalah detrimental to traditional Judaism and guilty of severing the bond between the Jewish community and the yeshivoth. He met the challenge of the Haskalah by establishing hundreds of yeshivoth to train dedicated spiritual and communal leaders who would again close the gap between yeshivoth and Jewish communal life.[85]

Rabbi Nathan Zvi Finkel

Another outstanding representative of the Musar Movement who tried to avoid public confrontation with the Maskilim was Rabbi Nathan Zvi Finkel of the Slobodca school of musar. Rabbi Finkel also vehemently disliked the Haskalah movement.[86]

If he suspected anyone of reading (even glancing) at anything even hinting of the Haskalah, he did not want him

---

[84]See Rabbi Joseph Yozel Hurwitz, *Matragath ha-Adam* (Jerusalem, 1964), I, p. 18f.

[85]*Ibid.*, p. 19.

[86]Interview with Mr. Joseph Freedman of Asbury Park, N.J., who began to study under Rabbi Finkel in 1894, considered the oldest surviving student of Slobodca. Also Rabbi Jacob Lesin, masgiah ruchni of Rabbi Isaac Elhanan Theological Seminary, and a former student of Rabbi Finkel, confirmed the above information in an interview.

in the Beth Midrash. He felt it was contagious like a disease to keep him in the same place where other bahurim (students) were. A boy was once observed reading *Te'udah be-Israel* by Isaac Baer Levinsohn and was asked henceforth to do his learning in another place. . . ."[87]

The book *Te'udah be-Israel* (*Instruction in Israel*) endeavored, without trespassing the boundaries of traditional Judaism, to depict the following truths by citing examples from Jewish history and sayings of great authorities:

1. The Jew is obligated to study the Bible as well as Hebrew grammar and to interpret the Biblical text in accordance with the plain grammatical sense.

2. The Jewish religion does not condemn the knowledge of foreign languages and literature, especially of the languages of the country, such knowledge being required both in the personal interest of the individual Jew and in the common interest of the Jewish people.

3. The study of secular sciences is not attended by any danger for Judaism, men of the type of Maimonides having remained loyal Jews, in spite of their extensive general culture.

4. It is necessary from the economic point of view to strengthen productive labor, such as handicrafts and agriculture, at the expense of commerce and brokerage, also to discourage early marriages between persons who are unprovided for and have no definite occupation.[88]

Since Rabbi Finkel was involved in the establishment of a kollel in Kovna for the study of musar, where some of the students practiced asceticism, he was berated by the Maskilim.[89] He could not accept the Haskalah because it threatened the survival of traditional Judaism. Even the reading of *Te'udah be-Israel* implied that the poison could be spread and so must be checked immediately, without examining the contradictions or enlightened views of the contents of the book. The Maskilim could not accept the Kovna

---

[87]Interview with Mr. Joseph Freedman (quote).

[88]See Isaac Baer Levinsohn, *Te'udah be-Israel* in S. M. Dubnow, *History of the Jews in Russia and Poland*, translated by I. Friedlaender (Philadelphia, Jewish Publication Society, 1918), II, p. 126.

[89]See Moses Joshua Levin, "Nazirei Israel," *op. cit.* See also *Sefer ha-Zichronoth*, *op. cit.*, pp. 129-131.

kollel because they felt a movement that discouraged Haskalah must be backward and parasitic. Yes, the lack of communication, tolerance, and unity was the order of a day which divided many Jews into two camps, the camp of Haskalah and the camp of musar.

CHAPTER 4

THE MUSAR MOVEMENT VERSUS THE TSARIST GOVERNMENT

Rabbi Israel Salanter and his disciples participated actively in the struggle of the Jews against the Tsarist government. Rabbi Salanter organized a special committee of students and friends to find solutions to such problems as the canton system, the confinement of Jews within the Pale of Settlement, and many others. The committee consisted of his pupil and son-in-law Rabbi Elijahu Eliezer Grodzenski of Vilna, his pupil Rabbi Elijahu Levensohn of Kartinga, his disciple Rabbi Hillel Milikovski of Amitzislav, and Rabbis Elhanan Cohen and Zev Smilke Cohen of Vitevsk. The brothers Meir and Leib Friedland, rich merchants in St. Petersburg, were also members of the committee.[1]

Rabbi Elhanan Cohen Lobbies

In 1851, Rabbi Salanter dispatched Rabbi Elhanan Cohen to St. Petersburg to devote himself to the problems confronting the Jews—in particular, that of military conscription. Rabbi Elijahu Levensohn donated 1,110 rubles to support Rabbi Cohen's lobbying efforts.[2] Rabbi Cohen stayed in St. Petersburg until 1879, working for Jewish welfare. He was able to contact many ministers of the Tsarist regime as well as distinguished Jewish personalities such as Baron Gunzburg and Poliyakov. He was active in the abolishment of many decrees against the Jews.[3] When Rabbi Cohen passed away in 1881, Baron Gunzburg and Poliyakov called a meeting to discuss antisemitic outbursts. At the meeting the treasurer of the organization for spreading the Enlightenment, Leon Rosenthal, stood up and said, "The reason for the antisemitic outbursts against our people is our inability to find a suitable successor for Rabbi Elhanan Cohen, who could have prevented the evil if he were alive. . . ."[4]

---

[1]Dov Katz, *Tenuath ha-Musar* (Tel Aviv, 1952), I, 202.
[2]Jacob Lipschitz, *Sichron Jacob* (Kovna, 1924), I, 166.
[3]*Ibid.*, p. 172. See also Dov Katz, *op. cit.*, I, 20.
[4]Jacob Lipschitz, *op. cit.*, p. 172.

Rabbi Cohen had been in close touch with Rabbi Salanter and made no move without his consent.[5] As time passed, Rabbi Aharon Nevizki was appointed by Rabbi Salanter and his aides to lobby in behalf of the Jews. On occasion, Rabbi Hillel Milikovsky, Rabbi Zev Cohen, and others went to St. Petersburg and stayed there for many months.

Mistakes of the Maskilim

The followers of the Enlightenment began writing against the Talmud and against the traditional Jewish method of education. There were those who wrote letters to the government asking its intervention in bringing the Enlightenment to the Jews, in constructing government-sponsored schools in every city, in exiling the Hasidic rabbis, in removing rabbis and Torah scholars from their positions and replacing them with German rabbis holding college degrees, in abolishing Jewish courts, in forcing the Jews to change their mode of apparel, in taking away privileges from religious teachers, and in limiting the publishing of religious books.[6]

The Russian Mendelssohn, Isaac Baer Levinsohn (1788-1860) concludes, in his book *Bet Yehudah* (*The House of Judah*) his historic review of Judaism with a eulogy of the government of Nicholas I for its kindness toward the Jews and for its agreement in following the plan of reform suggested to it, namely: to open elementary schools for the instruction of Russian and mathematics as well as Hebrew and the commands of the Jewish faith, and to set up institutions of higher rabbinical learning in the larger cities; to establish the office of Chief Rabbi, with a supreme council under him, which should have power over Jewish spiritual and communal affairs in Russia; to allot to a third of the Jewish population parcels of land for agricultural endeavors, and to restrict luxury in dress and furniture in which even the improverished classes attempted to indulge.[7]

In 1840, the Maskilim of Vilna responded to Minister of Education Uvarov's plans in a letter in which the following four reforms were stressed:

[5]Dov Katz, *op. cit.*, p. 203.
[6]Jacob Lipschitz, *op. cit.*, pp. 84, 138.
[7]Isaac Baer Levinsohn, *Bet Yehudah* (*The House of Judah*), ch. 146.

1. The transformation of the rabbinate through the establishment of rabbinical seminaries, the appointment
   of graduates from German universities as rabbis, and
   the formation of consistories after the pattern of Western Europe.
2. The reform of school education through the opening
   of secular schools after the model of Odessa and Riga
   and the training of new teachers from among the Maskilim.
3. The struggle with the proponents of obscurantism,
   who stifled every endeavor for popular enlightenment.
4. The improvement of Jewish economic life by intensify-
   ing agricultural colonization, the establishment of
   technical and arts and crafts schools, and similar measures.[8]

Several years later, the writers of this circular letter became
disillusioned with the "benevolent intentions" of the government.
This, however, was not enough to rectify the biggest mistake of the
Enlightenment—its constant willingness to rely upon the support
of "enlightened absolutism." The intolerance of the Orthodox rabbis and the uneducated masses influenced the handful of Maskilim
toward those who, in the eyes of the Jewish population, were the
source of its tragedy. Indeed, this incongruity resulted in tears and
sorrow.

The government of Nicholas I responded to the wishes of the
Maskilim by passing decrees which proved to be really detrimental
to traditional Judaism. For instance, in 1844 legislation was passed
changing the Jews' traditional garb, prohibiting the study of the
Talmud and Hebrew grammar in religious schools, limiting the
publishing of religious books, and abolishing the privileges of the
rabbis. In 1855, a law was signed by the Tsar prohibiting religious
teachers from teaching without a high school or seminary diploma.
All of these decrees were intended to uproot traditional Judaism
and to facilitate assimilation.

Rabbi Salanter led a group of lobbyists[9] for thirty-eight years in
an attempt to abolish these decrees. This lobbying was effective in

---

[8]S. M. Dubnow, *op. cit.,* pp. 136f.
[9]Rabbi Hillel Milikovsky, Rabbi Elijahu Levinsohn, Rabbi Elijahu Eliezer
Grodzenski, Rabbi Benush Katznelson, Rabbi Lev Friedland, Dr. Hirsenhorn.

that it caused a gradual annulment of the restrictions; in particular, it prevented the closing of religious schools. In 1893, Tsar Alexander III was persuaded by the lobbyists to issue a decree requiring a religious teacher to pay three rubles for a teaching license without having to take an examination in secular knowledge.[10]

Lobbying from Germany

When Rabbi Salanter left Russia for Germany, he continued to take an interest in the affairs of Russian Jews through correspondence with their communal leaders. Settling in Germany enabled him to inform other parts of the world of the plight of the Jews without fear, so that public opinion might try to seek privileges for the Jews or provide financial aid. He made several trips from Germany to Vilna, Kovna, and St. Petersburg on matters regarding oppression of the Jews in Russia.

Lobbying on behalf of German Jews

While he was in Germany Rabbi Salanter was also involved in the governmental and communal affairs of German Jewry. He published articles in the "Israelite" in order to remove discriminations against the German Jews.

After the Franco-German War of 1870-1871, nationalism was the guiding principle in European politics. In nations with mixed populations, particularly in those settled by Magyars, Teutons, and Slavs, economics and politics were injected with a militant nationalism which excluded all those different in color, descent, and language. The very presence of a Jew caused a perturbing situation; he was denied entrance into the national ranks even though he longed to join them and was prepared to make great sacrifices on behalf of the national cause. The success of the Jew in the realm of economics was begrudged, even though he placed himself fully at the service of the national economy. Nationalism was held in check when retaliatory measures were anticipated, but the Jews, a scattered minority, were without the resources of a compact minority or the protection of a foreign power; therefore, no retaliatory measures were feared by those who made the Jews the object of discrimination.

---

[10] Jacob Lipschitz, op. cit., II, 134.

For periods of time the opposition was passive, only to become active at the opportune time. In Germany, such opportunities did occur, as a result of religious conflict and economic disillusionment. German Chancellor Otto von Bismarck's Kulturkampf, the age-old conflict between the State and the Roman Catholic Church, was countered by the Catholics with a campaign of the press against the Jewish people. An economic collapse was the result of the wild speculation which had infected German exchanges during years of industrial expansion, and a number of Jewish financiers were blamed for the overexpansion.

In 1879, the followers of Adolf Stocker formed the League of Antisemites, which set as its task the liberation of the German Fatherland from "complete Judaization" and the preservation of "tolerable existence" for the descendants of the original inhabitants. Rabbi Salanter in Germany was disturbed by the discriminations and was involved to some extent personally with high government officials, to remove them.[11]

Lobbying of Rabbi Elijahu Levensohn

One of Rabbi Salanter's students became very active in spreading abroad news of the horrors of the pogroms of 1881-1882 in Russia. He was Rabbi Elijahu Levensohn of Kartinga. He became a very prominent lobbyist on behalf of the Jewish people in Russia. As an international banker and businessman, Rabbi Levensohn made trips to Germany, France, England, and other countries, where he promulgated the sufferings of the Russian Jews, particularly in the pogroms.[12]

Rabbi Levensohn's lobbying in England on behalf of Russian Jewry was instrumental in stimulating a positive reaction on the part of English Jews to alleviate the persecutions of their brethren in Russia. The following is the text of the Memorial to the Tsar, voted on at the Guildhall meeting in 1882.

> We citizens of London respectfully approach your Majesty, and humbly beg your gracious leave to plead the cause of the afflicted. Cries of distress have reached us from

---

[11]This is based on the correspondence with Dr. Eberman in Dov Katz, *op. cit.*, II, 209. See also J. Mark, *op. cit.*, p. 88.
[12]See Dov Katz, *op. cit.*, II, 313.

thousands of suffering in your vast Empire; and we Englishmen, with pity in our souls for all who suffer, turn to your Majesty to implore for them your Sovereign aid and clemency.

Five millions of your Majesty's subjects groan beneath the yoke of exceptional and restrictive laws. Remnants of a race whence all religion sprang, ours and yours, and every creed on earth that owns one God—men who cling with all devotion to their ancient faith and forms of worship, these Hebrews are in your Empire subject to such laws that under them they cannot live and thrive.

Those laws built up in bygone times when intolerance was the rule in almost every state, have been intensified by later ordinances and weigh as grievous burdens on Hebrew subjects of your Majesty, raising a barrier between them and their Christian fellow-subjects, making them a pariah caste, degraded and despised as if an accursed race.

Pent up in narrow bounds within your Majesty's wide Empire and within these bounds forced to reside chiefly in towns that reek and overflow with every form of poverty and wretchedness, forbidden all free movement; hedged in every enterprise by restrictive laws; forbidden tenure of land, their means of livelihood have become so cramped as to tender life for them well-nigh impossible.[13]

The Memorial goes on to say that higher education was being denied to the Jewish people, except in limits far below the due proportions of their needs and desires. The Jews were not permitted to enter the professions, as were the other citizens of Russia. Jewish soldiers were denied promotion in the army, despite their great valor and merit. Small wonder that in the struggle against discrimination their faults and failings should come uppermost, hiding the many virtues of the Jews.

The Memorial insisted that Jews had virtues; and that Jews declared alien by law could still be patriots.

The Jews served in the Imperial Army out of all proportion; they fought with bravery; they shed blood for their country. The Jews were loyal to the Tsar. They contrived to obey the law even

---

[13]Jacob Lipschitz, "Memorial to the Tsar," op. cit., III, 44f.

though its burden was heavy, and true to the commands of the Torah, they prayed in their synagogues for the welfare of the Tsar's throne and home.[14]

The Memorial to the Tsar concludes with the following:

Sire. We who have learnt to tolerate all creeds, deeming it part of true religion to permit religious liberty, we beseech your Majesty to repeal those laws that afflict these Israelites. Give them the blessing of equality. In every land where Jews have equal rights, the nation prospers. We pray that you then annul those special laws and disabilities that crush and cow your Hebrew Subjects.

And mighty Sire. Permit the sunshine of your Imperial Grace to brighten their dark homes, and let them feel the warmth of your paternal favor. As every passing year your Majesty's vast Empire widens and grows, so enter a new sphere of conquest, proclaimed by this emancipation Emperor of five million hearts swelling with gratitude.

Sire. Your Royal Sister, our Empress Queen (whom God preserve) bases her throne upon her people's love, making their happiness her own. So may your Majesty gain from your subjects' love all strength and happiness, making your mighty Empire mightier still, rendering your throne firm and impregnable, reaping new blessings for your House and Home.[15]

---

[14]*Ibid.*, p. 48.
[15]*Ibid.*

CHAPTER 5

THE MUSAR MOVEMENT AND
THE JEWISH SOLDIER

The followers of the Musar Movement observed the Jewish soldier's experiences in the armies of Nicholas I and Alexander II. Voltaire's depiction of Prussia as a nation that did not have an army, as the army had the country, to some degree applies to the Russia of Tsar Nicholas I. The Empire, with a population of some sixty to seventy millions, cared for a force of over one million under arms.[1] Professor John Shelton Curtiss writes:

> Probably no contemporary army could equal it in the magnificence of its great parades, the masses of resplendent cavalry, or the perfection of a complicated system of drill and maneuver. Furthermore, it added to the glory won in the stubborn defense against Napoleon's Grande Armeé and its victorious march to Paris in 1814 by gaining new laurels through victories over Persians, Turks, Poles, and insurgent Magyars. It was by virtue of its prestige and power that for nearly thirty years Nicholas could play the role of gendarme of Europe.[2]

The army was the favorite agency of Nicholas I, who always wore a uniform, slept on a hard camp bed, and surrounded himself with soldiers. His aides, adjutants, and even his ministries came from the army. In the 1840's military men held ten of the thirteen ministerial portfolios, and it is reasonable to assume that Nicholas I would have filled the ministries of justice, education, and foreign affairs with generals, if he had found any competent of holding them.[3] Many of the soldiers holding positions in the

---

[1] J. S. Curtiss, "The Army of Nicholas I: Its Role and Character," *American Historical Review* (1958) Vol. 63, p. 880.
[2] *Ibid.*
[3] M. O. Gershenson, ed., *Epokha Nikolaia I* (Moscow, 1911), pp. 21-22.

bureaucracy were not field commanders, but rather court generals.[4]

Some 180,000 old soldiers unfit for regular duty formed the Internal Defense force.[5] They were stationed all over Russia, guarded banks and state institutions, including prisons, and accompanied convicts to places of confinement. (In St. Petersburg alone they did not perform these duties, since here the Guards regiments provided troops to guard state buildings and to maintain order in the capital.) The Internal Defense force did not always perform these duties well, for many of the old soldiers were not fit to catch lawbreakers or to stop riots. In France and Austria twenty or thirty thousand gendarmes and armed police carried out these tasks, while Russia used 180,000 to perform similar functions.[6]

The army was "quite effective in assimilating non-Russians into the Russian community." Nicholas I's Regime provided opportunities for noble youths from the Baltic states and Finland, Poland and Lithuania, Georgia and the mountain tribes of the Caucasus to enlist in military schools or to receive officer training through field service with the regiments.[7]

The Russian people found the army a burden, because of Russia's miserable communications, the nature of the serf system, and the enormous body of men under arms.[8] The army filled its ranks per thousand males.[9]

Military Despotism as a Means of De-Judaization

Nicholas I applied military despotism as a means of de-Judaization. A decree was passed that the customary exemption tax was void and that personal military service would be substituted. The term of service was extended to twenty-five years, and boys were the main target of the decree. S. M. Dubnow writes:

> Not satisfied with imposing a civil obligation upon a people deprived of civil rights, the Tsar desired to use the Rus-

---

[4]Mikhail A. Polievktov, *Nikolai I. Biografia i obzor tsarstvovaniia* (St. Petersburg, 1914), p. 321.

[5]J. S. Curtiss, *op. cit.*, p. 882.

[6]*Ibid.*

[7]*Svod Voennykh Postanovlenti* (5 pts. in 12, St. Petersburg, 1838), Pt. I, Bk. III, "Obrazovanie Voenno-Uchebnykh Zavedenii Ikh Upravleniiami."

[8]Rostislav A. Fadieev, *Vooruzhenniia Silly Rossii* (Moscow, 1868), p. 26f.

by drafting men of the lowest classes at the rate of five, six, or eight

[9]J. S. Curtiss, *op. cit.*, p. 882.

sian military service, a service marked by most extraordinary features, as an educational and disciplinary agency for his Jewish subjects: the barrack was to serve as a school, or rather as a factory, for producing a new generation of de-Judaized Jews, who were completely Russified, and if possible, Christianized.[10]

The recruiting decree of 1827 was discriminatory towards the Jews. Jews were horrified on reading the eighth clause of the law stating that "the Jewish conscripts presented by the Jewish communes shall be between ages twelve and twenty-five." This provision was supplemented by Clause 74: "Jewish minors, i.e., below the age of eighteen, shall be placed in preparatory establishments for military training."[11]

The canton system, the institution of minor recruits, applied also to Christians. The decree specified that children of Christian soldiers in active service were to be drafted. In the case of Jewish minors, the law referred to all Jewish families. It specified that Jewish minors' preparatory training "should not be included in the term of active service, the latter to start only with the age of eighteen (Clause 90)." It meant that Jewish minors were required to put in an additional term of six years beyond the obligatory twenty-five years. Another flagrant discrimination against Jewish conscripts was that "they be free from any disease or defect incompatible with military service, but the other qualifications required by the general rules shall be left out of consideration (Clause 10)."[12] The purpose of the Recruiting Ukase of 1827 was "to equalize military duty for all estates," without the provision for equal rights of all estates.

If the purpose of the law was to provide equal military service to all estates, the Russian Government did not have to pass a separate recruiting law for the Jews. The separate ukase for the Jews consisted of ninety-five clauses, with an additional sixty-two clauses, for the instruction of military and civil authorities. The Russian government had only to mention that the general laws of recruiting conscripts applied also to the Jews. Instead, the statement said: "The

---

[10]S. M. Dubnow, *History of The Jews in Poland and Russia* (Philadelphia, 1946), II, 15.
[11]*Ibid.*, p. 18.
[12]*Ibid.*, p. 19.

general laws and institutions are not valid in the case of the Jews (Clause 3)." The results of the separate Jewish recruiting law will be further discussed later.

The Kahals (Jewish communes) were responsible for conscripting the recruits. Each community was ordered to elect from three to six executive officers who were obligated to see that the community supply the given quota of recruits. If the community did not fulfill the given number, it would be forced by the authorities to provide the necessary number.

Rabbis, merchants holding membership in guilds, artisans affiliated with trade unions, agricultural colonists, factory mechanics, and graduates from a Russian educational institution were exempted from military service. Jews exempted from military duty were required to pay "recruiting money," one thousand rubles for each conscript. The general decree which stated that a "regular recruit could offer as his substitute a volunteer" was extended to the Jews, with the proviso that "the volunteer must be also a Jew."[13]

Nicholas I found a way to harm Judaism by touching one of the important pillars of Jewish life, the children. It is impossible to portray in words the agony and tragedy of parents whose sons left for the army. Before his departure the son had to go through the following ceremony as stipulated by the instruction to the civil authorities: "The recruit was to be arrayed in his prayer-shawl and shroud with his phylacteries wound around his arm; he should be placed before the Ark, amidst burning candles and to the accompaniment of shofar blasts, made to recite a lengthy awe-inspiring oath."[14] The oath was administered in Hebrew as well as in Russian. The conscript "was made to swear that he would faithfully perform his duties and obey his superiors as if he fought for the salvation of our land and our holy Torah."[15] After adding a statement that he had no mental reservations about his oath, the recruit concluded, "But if I shall sin, either of my own will or persuaded by someone else, and violate the oath which I am taking today faithfully to serve in the army I, together with my family, shall be excommunicated in this world and the world to come, Amen."[16] Professor Salo Baron writes the following:

---

[13]*Ibid.*, p. 20.

[14]*Ibid.*

[15]Salo Baron, *The Russian Jew under Tsars and Soviets* (New York, 1964), p. 35.

[16]Saul M. Ginsburg, *Historische Verk* (New York, 1937), II, 10.

Since most Jewish families knew what to expect, many youngsters of draft age fled to forests, mutilated their bodies so as to become physically ineligible, and resorted to all sort of subterfuges to evade the draft. The communal authorities, implacably pressed to meet their quotas, often employed so-called Khappers (Kidnappers) who seized the required number of youths on streets or by invading private homes. These ruthless agents often used such illegal methods as forcibly depriving of their certificates young men occupationally exempted from the draft. Most tragically, they often seized children aged eight or nine (one allegedly aged five) and claimed that they were twelve years or over.[17]

The author, in his research, came across the names of Jews who were captors of minors, and who discriminated against the poor.[18]

The Tragedy of the Young Conscripts

Alexander Herzen depicts the tragedy of the young conscripts. Herzen was expelled by the Russian government to the government of Vyatka in 1835 for "spreading liberal doctrines." By chance, he met on his way a group of Jewish recruits. He held the following conversation with the escorting offcer:

"Whom do you carry and to what place?"

---

[17]Salo Baron, *op. cit.*, p. 36.

[18]In the city of Ilia, in the region of Vilna, the author's parents, Chaja and Leib Eckman, lived from 1925-1939 as a married couple. Their parents and grandparents told them many stories about the Jewish Kidnappers. Before the two were married, each family searched the other's background to learn whether any relative had had anything to do with enforcing the required number of recruits. An outstanding pious rabbi for Ilia and surrounding towns excommunicated certain captors of minors for their relentless activities; the excommunication stressed limited years for their descendants. The grandparents of Chaja and Leib Eckman had had no connection with these horrors and so the two were married. They were, however, acquainted with families in Ilia whose grandparents were either Kidnappers or were closely associated with the hunting down of minors. The Kugal family, the Cinder family, the Heiken family—all were descendants of captors or of those who cooperated with the enforcing of Nicholas I's Recruiting Ukase. These families were discriminated against by other Jews when it came time for their children to be married; also some members of the families "died young." Chaja and Leib Eckman lived in Europe until 1949. They were eyewitnesses to the Russo-Japanese War, the First World War, and the Second World War. Leib Eckman passed away in 1974; his wife lives in Chelsea, Massachusetts. The above episode was related to the author by his parents.

"Well, sir, you see, they got together a bunch of these accursed Jewish youngsters between the age of eight and nine.
I suppose they are meant for the fleet, but how should I
know? At first the command was to drive them to Kazan.
I have had them on my hands for a hundred versts or there-
abouts. The officer that turned them over to me told me
they were an awful nuisance. A third of them remained on
the road (at this the officer pointed with his finger to the
ground). Half of them will not get to their destination."
"Epidemics, I suppose?" I inquired, stirred to the very
core. "No, not exactly epidemics; but they just fall like
flies. Well, you know, these Jewish boys are so puny and
delicate. They cannot stand mixing dirt for ten hours, with
dry biscuits to live on. Again everywhere strange folks, no
father, no mother, no caresses. Well, then, you just hear a
cough and the youngster is dead. Hello, corporal, get out
the small fry."[19]

The small children were gathered in a military line. According to Herzen, it was one of the most dreadful scenes that he ever
saw. These children, exposed to the wind of the Artic Ocean, were
confronting death. He told the officer, "Take good care of them."[20]

When the children arrived at their destination, Greek Orthodox clergy tried to give them spiritual guidance. The priests, however, were thwarted in their attempts. The sergeants and corporals
began to apply brutal methods of persuasion. Children were forced
every evening to get down on their knees for hours. Those who
were willing to accept baptism were allowed to go to sleep. Those
who rejected it were not allowed to sleep all night. Those who refused to eat pork or meals made with lard were left to starve. Others
were fed salted fish and afterwards were prevented from drinking
water. Only those who accepted the Greek Orthodox faith were allowed to drink water. The majority of the Jewish conscripts who
were not able to withstand the atrocities of "persuasion" saved themselves by conversion.

There were many conscripts between the ages of fifteen and
eighteen who accepted torture in the name of God and Judaism.

---

[19]S. M. Dubnow, op. cit., p. 25.
[20]Alexander Herzen, Byloe i Dumy, foreign edition, I, 308. See also S. M.
Dubnow, op. cit., p. 25.

Only a few of them were able to endure the senseless beatings, hunger and thirst, and sleeplessness.

The Tragedy of Adult Soldiers

Adult Jewish soldiers between ages eighteen and twenty-five were not exposed to the same methods of persuasion. They were drafted for twenty-five years and were sent to remote Christian places. Since many of them between the ages of eighteen and twenty-five were married, they gave divorces to their wives. The separation of the soldier from his wife, family, and the Jewish environment for a quarter of a century greatly facilitated conversion.

The adult Jewish soldier endured unbearable sufferings. He experienced physical beatings and ridicule because he was unable to express himself in Russian, was unwilling to eat nonkosher food, and had difficulty adjusting to the new environment and the military way of life. Conversion was the open door to a higher rank even to the well-oriented Jewish soldier.

The Statute on Military Service provided the right for Jewish soldiers of distinction in military service to join the civil service. In practice, however, conversion was the determining criterion for admission to the civil service. Many Jews who completed the service and even became invalids were prohibited from settling in the districts outside the Pale. Only during the reign of Alexander II were Jewish soldiers permitted to settle in the districts outside the Pale.

Such were the hardships and tribulations of the minors and adult soldiers of Nicholas I. They left stories of military martyrdom for future generations. The recruiting of minors and soldiers, however, left a strong impression upon Rabbi Israel Salanter and the followers of the Musar Movement.

Number of Jewish Victims of the Conscription

Records of the number of conversions are incomplete, but from those available we learn that "the percentage of converts was very high, in many instances reaching 100 percent."[21] In the battalions of Saratov in the year 1845, all the Jewish cantonists were baptized, including 130 who came in May and were forced to convert within two weeks. In the same year the Perm battalion reported similar

---

[21]Louis Greenberg, *The Jews In Russia* (New Haven, 1965), I, 51.

successes to the Holy Synod. These results were "due to the special pressure brought to bear upon the military and religious officials through the intensified program instituted by the Emperor in 1883.[22] In previous years the achievements had not been quite so satisfactory. For example, in the half battalion of Verkhne-Uralsk, only one third of the Jewish children were won over to baptism between the years 1836-42, and the battalion of Saratov, which reported such perfect results in 1845, converted only 687 recruits out of its 1,304 Jewish conscripts during the years 1828-1842.[23]

Professor Salo Baron writes the following regarding the number of Jewish victims of the conscription from 1827-1856

> We have no definite information about the total number of Jewish victims of the Rekruchina (recruiting) while it lasted—from 1827 to 1856. According to some records, 26,279 were drafted in 11 years. Another estimate mentions some 40,000 in the first 17 years. The total may indeed not have exceeded 60,000 in the entire 30-year period. The Jewish population, which at the time may have averaged some 3,000,000, could sustain such losses without serious interruption in its numerical expansion.[24]

The Musar Movement's Involvement on Behalf of the Jewish Soldier The Reign of Nicholas I

We have seen previously how Rabbi Salanter's followers lobbied in St. Petersburg and elsewhere on behalf of their fellow Jews. Rabbi Salanter himself devoted much of his own time and effort in attempting to abolish the recruiting decree of 1827. The inhuman ukase affected him deeply; he complained that it made his life miserable. He organized many trips to high-ranking officials. Nothing stood in his way. Once it became known that an important high officer did not favor the order, Rabbi Salanter traveled to see this officer, who might be urged to persuade the Tsar to annul it.[25] At the same time, he and his followers discredited Jewish leaders who were engaged in wrenching children from their mothers' arms, who

---

[22]*Ibid.*
[23]Saul M. Ginsburg, *op. cit.*, III, pp. 63, 102.
[24]Salo Baron, *op. cit.*, p. 37.
[25]This was told by Rabbi A. Broida in the name of Rabbi Naphtali Amsterdam in Dov Katz, *Tenuath ba-Musar, op. cit.*, I, 204.

were in a position to help their unfortunate fellow Jews, but did nothing.

Rabbi Salanter had an ethical approach to communal problems. In the city of Salant, the birthplace of Rabbi Salanter, a child was snatched for military conscription from a poor widow, who had come from elsewhere to ask for charity. The shouts and cries of the widow reached Rabbi Salanter, who was in Salant at the time. The widow pleaded with him to intercede for the return of her son.[26]

> After reciting the blessing over wine, Rabbi Salanter rose suddenly from his seat with great anger, and began to attack the people surrounding him concerning the kidnapping, accusing them of being murderers. . . . As he was personally acquainted with the leaders of the community, he berated each leader separately. To one he said: "You are righteous by not carrying your handkerchief on the Sabbath, but kidnapping a person and selling him does not bother you? To a second he said: You are cautious with an easy deed as well as a hard deed; but to turn over a soul of Israel for conversion is permissible?" To a third he remarked: "You are careful with a ritual . . . you are not, however, afraid to transgress the command of not oppressing a widow and an orphan?" And thus spoke Salanter to the fourth and to the fifth—the congregants were astounded and could not answer him. Rabbi Salanter left the city that Sabbath afternoon. The shameful rebuke of Rabbi Israel Salanter . . . and his immediate departure from the city embarrassed the leaders greatly. Also the leaders responsible for the matter recognized their malice and decided to free the child to appease the Rabbi. . . .[27]

Rabbi Elijahu Levensohn of Kartinga, who was also in Salant at that time, informed Rabbi Salanter that the boy was returned to his widowed mother, should Rabbi Salanter decide to come back to Salant. . . .[28]

A similar incident occurred in Kovna. A poor woman whose

---

[26]Told by Rabbi Jacob Berman in the name of his ancestors of Salant in Dov Katz, *Tenuath ha-Musar*, op. cit., I, p. 204.
[27]*Ibid.*
[28]*Ibid.*

son was snatched came to the synagogue where Rabbi Salanter prayed on the Sabbath. Men attempted to force her to leave the premises, but Rabbi Salanter came to her defense. He criticized people "whose hearts are like stone and who do not feel the agonies of people at all."[29] When Rabbi Salanter heard the news of the abolishment of the child-military-service ukase, he declared a holiday.[30]

Nicholas I's military system, which stressed unthinking obedience and parade-ground convolutions, produced ill-prepared commanders in time of war. Only the Caucasus army's young generals disregarded to some extent the spit and polish soldiering. Higher military officials regarded these generals as unfit for normal military combat, thus denying them high commands. In the Crimean War (1854-1856), Nicholas relied on elderly and ineffective generals, such as Paskevich, M. D. Gorchkov, Prince Menshikov, and Count Osten-Sacken, who failed miserably. The incompetence at the top handicapped the production of necessary implements of war. Outdated weapons, inflexibility of the system in wartime, poor logistics, disease, and corruption proved the army to be a failure in the Crimean War.

Professor Curtiss writes:
It is clear, then, that the Russian army under Nicholas was less effective than its glitter and its vast numbers would indicate. While it was strong enough to repress all peasants' revolts at home, it proved less successful against foreign foes. Above all, the burdens that the army imposed on the nation were not in proportion to its value. It seems safe to say that the strengths and weaknesses of the army reflected those of Russian society. It had the numbers and the endurance of a virile and unsophisticated people. Its weaknesses, complicated by the pedantic policy of the emperor, were those of a backward serf system that lacked industrial and commercial techniques. Vast social and economic changes would have to occur before Russia could have an effective army.[31]

29Told by Rabbi A. Broida in the name of Rabbi Naphtali Amsterdam in Dov Katz, *Tenuath ha-Musar*, op. cit., I, p. 205f.

30*Ibid.*

31John S. Curtiss, *op. cit.*, p. 889.

The Reign Of Alexander II

The Crimean War exposed the weaknesses of the army of Nicholas I, because it was badly beaten by the Turks. The defeat of Nicholas' army had proved that the sheer weight of manpower and perfection of drilling, so impressive on parade grounds, was no substitute for modernized equipment, organization, and training. Of some 2,200,000 man called to the colors by 1856, a mere fraction took active part in the fighting. The ruinous cost of maintaining this huge force and its failure to prevent the disastrous outcome of the war pointed to the necessity of fundamental army reforms.[32]

Alexander II, known in Russia as the liberator of the peasants, appointed General Dimitry Miliutin to reorganize the army. He served as Minister of War from 1861-1881. The general was a man of "vision and views." The army reorganization was done by General Miliutin with thoroughness. He introduced reforms such as the general staff, the medical service, army engineers, the territorial distribution of troops, the commissariat, military courts, the liberal arts program at the military schools, and up-to-date arms and equipment.[33] The most important contributions, however, were the "humanization of discipline, the betterment of conditions of service, and the introduction of conscription borne equally by all social classes.[34]

The conscription law of January 1, 1874, demanded that every able-bodied man at the age of twenty, irrespective of his social status, enter the service. The normal term of active service was six years, with nine years in the reserve and five years in the militia. The reserve and the militia were called up only in an emergency. The law did not draft all males of twenty. Breadwinners and "only sons" could be drafted only by the order of the Tsar. The term of military service for graduates from military schools was cut to four years; for those of secondary schools, to three years or to eighteen months, according to the class of the instruction; and for graduates from higher schools, to six months. Graduates from higher schools, however, were able to enter as volunteers, which shortened their

---

[32]Florinsky, M. A History and an Interpretation (New York, 1964), II, p. 906f.
[33]Ibid.
[34]Ibid.

term of service to three months.[35] The reforms removed some of the worst remnants of Russian medievalism.

A Committee of Jewish Affairs requested Alexander II to change the method of Jewish recruiting. The Coronation Manifesto of 1856 abolished the conscription of juveniles and stated the following:

1. Conscripts from the Jews are be taken in the same manner as from the other estates, especially those who are unsettled and are unemployed.
2. The recruiting from other estates and of males under age is void.
3. The general laws are applicable to the Jews in making up the shortage of conscripts.
4. The rules granting Jewish communities and Jewish individuals the right of replacing in their stead Jews seized without passports are to be abrogated.[36]

The general recruiting laws were now applicable to Jews and Christians. There were, however, some discriminations, such as increasing the conscripts from among those unsettled and not engaged in productive labor; also no Jew was allowed to be promoted beyond the rank of sergeant.

Representatives of the Musar Movement were perturbed by the conscription law of 1874. In 1879, Rabbi Salanter wrote an article in *Ha-Meliz* which portrayed his grief as a result of the government's complaint that Jewish youth of military age failed to report for duty, as well as for the chaotic conditions within the Jewish community in reference to birth certificates and ignorance in the details of the law.[37] Rabbi Salanter urged the leaders of the Jewish communities to explain to the Jews the details of the requirements of the law and to encourage them to obtain birth certificates indicating their correct age. He was disturbed that there were incidents in which some recruits had to serve in the army twice because of registration in more than one place. Also, more

---

[35]See the details of the conscription law of 1874 in *Ha-Carmel*, 1874, pp. 398-455. It appears that *Ha-Carmel* published the manifesto to inform its readers, thus it is a valuable, detailed account of the recruitment law of 1874. See also Florinsky, *op. cit.*, p. 908.

[36]See Dubnow, *op. cit.*, II, 156.

[37]See Israel Salanter, "Ma'orerr Ha-Nirtamim" in *Ha-Meliz* 8, 1879, 149-154.

Jewish recruits were conscripted than the law really required.[38] Rabbi Salanter held that the main reason for some youths dodging the draft was the evidence that they might be drafted into the army twice. Thus, they reasoned that if they were to be drafted into the army twice, it would be better to avoid the draft completely. However, according to Rabbi Salanter, more than one registration was responsible for drafting a youth twice.[39]

Although Rabbi Salanter lived at that time in Germany, he manifested his concern for the Jewish soldier in the Russian army. It appears that he did not object so much to the law itself, since it applied to all citizens of Russia regardless of race and social status, but rather at the misconceptions and misinterpretation of the details of the law on the part of the Jews.

Rabbis Simhah Zissel, Nathan Finkel, and Joseph Hurwitz, though concerned with the hardships and tribulations of Jewish soldiers in the army, nevertheless did not participate in the problems of the Jewish soldier because their interests and energies were channeled in the direction of Torah study and musar schools. Of course, among the Musar Movement's representatives who became best known for his involvement in behalf the Jewish soldier was Rabbi Israel Meir Kagan (1838-1933).

The Book of Rabbi Israel Meir Kagan concerning the Jewish Soldier

Rabbi Israel Meir Kagan was very disturbed by the new general recruiting law of 1874 because yeshiva students were now also eligible for the draft. Five or six religious men might be drafted from a town. The religious recruits who did not have a secular education were required to serve six years. They were sent to remote locations in Russia proper and to Siberia. Rabbi Kagan lamented, because he feared that thousands and tens of thousands of Jewish soldiers would be exposed to Russification, assimilation, forbidden foods and laxity in observance of the laws of the Torah.[40] Also the new recruiting law caused pain to Rabbi Kagan because it engendered delay in marriage. Before the new army law, marriage took place between the ages of eighteen and twenty. Now, parents de-

---

[38]*Ibid.*, p. 149.
[39]*Ibid.*
[40]Israel Meir Kagan, *Michtavei Hafets Hayyim* (New York, 1953), I, p. 18.

cided to marry off their daughters and sons after the males fulfilled six years of military duty. The fact that a single Jewish soldier was in an environment of Christian women was an ideal situation for intermarriage, which is prohibited by the Torah.[41]

Rabbi Kagan decided to promulgate an article urging the Jews to marry before entering the army. He reasoned that a married soldier with a family would abstain from forbidden sexual activity and intermarriage. The Russian government censured his article and stated: "It is better for the government to accept unmarried men in the army." The article was published in Prussia, and many Jews, including some outstanding rabbis, disagreed with the early-marriage proposal. The famous Malbim,[42] Rabbi Meir Loeb ben Jehiel Michael, (1809-1879) refused to give Rabbi Kagan his approval of the article, which indicates his disagreement with the proposal. Rabbi Kagan, however, was convinced that he was right in advocating early marriage and years later Jews began to marry off their children young again.

In 1881, Rabbi Kagan published *Mahaneh Israel* (*The Camp of Israel*). The purpose of the book was to provide a religious and moral code to the Jewish soldier in remote places. The book was only an introduction to Rabbi Kagan's relentless determination to improve the lot of the Jewish soldier. He wrote:

> Behold, if we look attentively at the present-day observance of the precepts of the Torah in this world, it is very lax even for settled Jews and in particular more so for Jewish soldiers; there are those among them who transgress the laws of the Torah with contempt; there are others who violate the laws for which the Torah commanded martyrdom."[43]

The paramount cause for laxity in keeping the commands of the Torah is the lack of knowledge of the Torah on the part of the soldier. Joseph Karo's Code of Jewish Law contains some laws which are different for soldiers than for others, taking into consideration the differences in location and time. The different laws can be lo-

---

[41]*Ibid.*

[42]Malbim wrote a commentary on the Bible characterized by a fine perception of the niceties of the Hebrew language.

[43]See Israel Meir Kagan, *Mahaneh Israel* (New York, 1943), p. 7.

cated in the Code; however, they require research in the primary sources. Many soldiers were stationed in places which did not have a learned man to answer for them the simple questions which require research. Rabbi Kagan concluded:

> Therefore, I found it necessary to prepare a code for soldiers based on the sources and I searched in detail to discover a certain decree . . . which will make it easier for soldiers to keep the law; and I also investigated the morals for every man in general and for soldiers in particular, whose morals, if corrupted, can bring disgrace to God. May God merit us to keep His Torah and its precepts and the commands between man and God and those commands between man and man. . . .[44]

There were other causes for laxity in keeping the precepts of the Torah. Some soldiers felt that the new environment caused them to violate certain commands; and that God had separated them from the rest of the precepts of the Torah. There were certain soldiers who were lax in the practice of the laws of the Torah because of the influence of irreligious friends in the army.[45]

God does not separate the sinning soldier from the rest of the Jews. The irreligious soldier remains as God's portion in his military dispersion to remote non-Jewish environments. Great is the merit of the soldier who keeps the laws of the Torah in the trying days of army life. The soldier will be inspired to be strong in his practice of Judaism by constantly recalling the trials of Abraham and Joseph in behalf of God.

Rabbi Kagan stressed the importance of prayer, fringes, phylacteries and the study of Torah. Prayer, he said, is greater than good deeds and sacrifices. Every Jewish soldier must take phylacteries along with him to the army. In case one of his phylacteries is lost, and he cannot borrow phylacteries from a friend, the soldier may put on one of the phylacteries. He must be careful to wear fringes in the army because they represent the numerical value of the 613 commands of the Torah. The putting on of fringes adds holiness to a Jew and prevents him from committing transgressions.

He further stressed that a soldier should devote some time to the

---

[44]*Ibid.*, p. 8.
[45]*Ibid.*, p. 15f.

study of Torah. This fulfills the precept of studying the Torah, which is applicable at all times; the study of Torah will inform the soldier the better to carry out the commands of the Torah; being engrossed in the study of Torah, the soldier will stay away from trouble, such as gossip, quarrel, and engaging in fraud; and a soldier should study Torah in order to set an example for other soldiers to emulate.[46]

Rabbi Kagan pointed out that the study of Torah would in the beginning engender mockery by non-Jewish soldiers and even some Jewish soldiers. Despite the derision, the Jewish soldier must strengthen himself and continue to study and to observe. Rabbi Moses Isserles wrote in the sixteenth century: "A person must disregard mockery in the cause of serving God." Great is the reward of a soldier who accepts ridicule in his determination to serve God and keep the practices of the Torah. If derision overtakes the soldier, laxity in the study of Torah will lead to other trespasses. The soldiers of non-Jewish belief and some Jews will mock him in putting on phylacteries, fringes and other daily practices. In the end, the sensitivity to derision will remove the yoke of the Torah; and the soldier will become a flagrant sinner.

Rabbi Kagan wrote that a soldier studying Torah would be highly respected by his commander, because the commander would know that he is not a thief, a drunkard, or a troublemaker. In the end, the mockery would stop, and he would be able to continue his study of Torah and practice of the commands without ridicule.[47]

The following incident is told by Rabbi Kagan:

> A religious soldier asked his commander for a leave on an army holiday. The commander permitted the pious soldier furlough for the day. He went to a certain house on the base to study Torah. By chance, the commander walked into the same house and saw the soldier studying with great enthusiasm. The commander was bewildered and told him, "I thought that when you asked me to excuse you for the day it was intended to go with the other soldiers to celebrate in the taverns." The soldier replied: "Believe me, my commander, the day that I am engrossed in the study of the Torah of God, is a day of great joy in my life

---

[46]*Ibid.*, p. 39f.
[47]*Ibid.*, p. 39f.

and a day of purpose in my life." The soldier related to his commander the morals of the Torah and the commander was very impressed by the answer of his religious soldier. The commander informed other commanders of the righteousness and morality of the Jewish soldier.[48]

The soldiers were urged to study practical matters. If a person cannot learn the laws by himself, said Rabbi Kagan, he shall study them with a group. If a soldier cannot grasp the study of law, he shall at least recite Psalms and shall not waste time.

The observance of the Sabbath and all its pertaining laws were emphasized in detail. The Sabbath is the big sign and covenant between God and the Jews. The Torah warned the Jew twelve times to keep the Sabbath holy. A person who observes the Sabbath is as if he keeps the whole Torah, according to the Sages.

The Jewish soldier is prohibited from eating forbidden food. A soldier who abstains from forbidden food at the table is considered to have carried out a positive command of the Torah. Holiness is continued by keeping the laws concerning forbidden food. Great is the merit of a soldier who observes the dietary laws in the name of God and Torah.

Hope is of paramount importance to a soldier; and it is a source of strength to a soldier in time of battle. He must hope in God to help him in time of war. Hope and confidence must be shared with fellow soldiers by emulating the example of Jonathan's inspiration to David in time of trouble.[49]

If a soldier returns safely from battle, he shall more so be grateful to God; and he shall recite a prayer to God for saving his life. If a soldier is taken captive by the enemy, he must retain his hope in God that he will be set free in the future.

Humility and loving-kindness are required of a Jewish soldier. A Jewish soldier must comport himself with humility, understanding, and loving-kindness to fellow soldiers. Give and take should be the relationship between soldiers. In three things loving-kindness is greater than charity, the Rabbis said: "Charity is with money, loving-kindness is with money and with the body; charity is given to the poor, loving-kindness is given to the poor and to the

---

[48]*Ibid.*, p. 41ff.
[49]*Ibid.*, p. 65.

rich; and loving-kindness enables a person to enjoy the fruits of this world, while the stock remains for him for the world to come.[50]

Gossip and informing are prohibited by the Torah. Jewish soldiers must be careful in their talk in order to avoid gossip and slander. Gossip and informing can cause non-Jewish soldiers to mock Jews. Soldiers should deter themselves from a quarrel because an altercation can cause slander and ridicule by non-Jewish soldiers. Consequently, strife by Jews and mockery by non-Jews lead to the desecration of the name of God. Great is the merit of a person who does not answer his friend in the time of a dispute, which will bring harmony, as the Sages said: "Because of harmony the world exists."[51]

Drunkenness, gambling, and trespass of sex laws are prohibited to the soldier. A Jewish soldier must observe the laws of the Torah and must control his temptation for gambling, women, and drunkenness.

The book *Mahaneh Israel* spread among the Jewish soldiers. The soldiers began to gather a quorum for prayer; they began to practice loving-kindness to each other; some soldiers began to write books dealing with Torah; they kept the Sabbath as much as possible; and they abstained from prohibitions of the Torah.[52] Many of the soldiers wrote to Rabbi Kagan of the utility of the book and how the book helped them to be God-fearing and pious Jews.[53]

During the Russo-Japanese War, Rabbi Kagan sent to soldiers important chapters of the book. A Jewish soldier relates the following incident:

> During the Russo-Japanese War, the book saved me many times from death. Once the commander saw me and some friends studying pamphlets of the book. The commander began to scream, "Don't you know that in a few hours we shall attack the enemy, and in such a danger you waste time with books of vanity? Pray to God for your lives." One

---

[50]*Ibid.*, p. 103.

[51]Talmud tractate *Chulin* 89.

[52]See *Michtavei Hafets Hayyim, op. cit.*, p. 20.

[53]*Ibid.* Leib Eckman, the father of the author, told him that three of his friends served in the Russo-Japanese War. They were observant in the precepts of the Torah during their duty in the army. The book *Mahaneh Israel* was of great usefulness to them in the army. The following three friends of Leib Eckman served in the Russo-Japanese War: Velvel Edelman, Jacob Dogsiski, who lived in Ilia, near Vilna, and who were both killed by the Nazis in 1943; and Leib Dworkin, who lived in Radiskowitz, a city near Ilia, and who now lives in Israel.

of us answered the commander, "My master, we are not wasting time, for the pages contain prayers and requests to God; without them we are weak.[54]

Rabbi Kagan went from city to city to collect money in order to provide kosher food for the soldiers. After a difficult discussion with the commanders of the Jewish soldiers, Rabbi Kagan and his committee obtained permission to establish three centers to obtain kosher food. Since many soldiers were in the vicinities of Vilna, Grodno, and Oran, committees there distributed kosher food to the soldiers.[55]

In 1923 Rabbi Kagan published an article in the newspaper "Der Yud" calling for kosher food for Jewish soldiers. He wrote the following:

> Everyone has to know that a soldier of the Jewish faith did not become lax in his keeping of the Torah; and he is obligated to keep the whole Torah as the other Jew. . . . Since the government does not force the Jewish soldier to eat forbidden foods, therefore Jews are responsible for helping them obtain kosher food. . . .[56]

In other words, every Jew is responsible for providing money to buy kosher food for a soldier—because one Jew is responsible for his fellow Jew. The rabbis said: "Everyone who shows kindness for human beings is rewarded by God."[57]

In conclusion, the book *Mahaneh Israel* is a unique legal and moral code because it was concerned with the religious, social, moral, and even economic problems of the Jewish soldier. It was the first book to deal in detail with the problems of the soldier. Of course, Karo deals with the problems of soldiers in the general context of Jewish law. No specific code, however, was available until Rabbi Israel Meir Kagan felt it was necessary to write one.

Rabbi Kagan manifests in the book a remarkable understanding of the soldier's religious, social, and economic problems. He was an eyewitness to their trials and tribulations, and he felt these

---

[54]*Ibid.*
[55]See *Michtavei Hafets Hayyim, op. cit.,* p. 21.
[56]See Israel Meir Kagan, "Kosher Essen far Yuddishe Zelner" in *Michtavei Hafets Hayyim, Ibid.,* p. 199f.
[57]*Ibid.*

deeply. He won the respect and confidence of the Jewish soldiers because he wrote a book on their behalf and participated in person in bringing them kosher food. Thus, Rabbi Kagan joined the select company of Rabbi Israel Salanter in improving the spiritual, moral, and economic life of the Jewish soldier.

The Haskalah's Attitude to the Conscription Law of 1874

In addition to the Musar Movement's reaction to the conscription law of 1874, the author found valuable primary sources depicting the attitude of the Haskalah toward the conscription decree of 1874. The Haskalah Movement in general looked upon the conscription law of 1874 as a law of social justice, since no particular class or ethnic group was exempt from it. Naturally, the Maskilim were not concerned with the religious problems of the Jewish soldier which perturbed the Musar Movement in general and Rabbis Salanter and Kagan in particular.

One of the most important spokesmen of the Haskalah concerning religious, social, and political issues was Moses Lilienblum. Moses Lilienblum held that the conscription law of 1874 was just, because no class or ethnic group was exempt from military recruitment. He condemned the richer Jews for bribing the physicians so that their sons would fail the physical, thus causing the increase of recruitment among the sons of the poor in order to meet the necessary quota of a district.[58] Lilienblum felt that the law provided the opportunity for the sons of the rich and the poor to learn to live together, to fight together and to overcome social prejudices. Surely, the richer soldiers would find more hardship and tribulation in their adjustment to army life than the poorer ones, because of the better living conditions at home. On the other hand, the poor soldiers' lot could not be worse than at home.

The Maskil Naphtali Herz Leib Lutzevski echoed the fairness of the conscription law of 1874 and berated those Jews who tried to dodge the draft through bribing the doctors. However, he asked the question, "Are the Jews alone guilty of bribing doctors and escaping the draft? The Russians are guilty of the same evils and no one condemns them, but when an incident occurs among the

---

[58]See Moses Lilienblum, "Nefesh Tahath Nefesh" in *Ha-Meliz* 1878, 75-80.

Jews, the government, the Russian people and even the Jews decry it."[59]

Both the Musar Movement and the Haskalah were concerned with the fate of the Jewish soldier in the Tsarist army. Both movements saw justice in the conscription law of 1874 since both could not accept the fact that in previous years the poor had to serve in place of the rich. Only in the realm of religion did the Musar Movement manifest greater concern, since it held that a soldier must keep the precepts of the Torah regardless of his hardships and tribulations. To the Haskalah Movement, of course, religious observance was not a concern.

---

[59]See Naphtali Herz Leib Lutzevski, "Hashkafah Al Matzav Achenu Bnei Israel Hahomri V'Hamusari" in *Ha-Magid*, 7, 1874, 44-45; 54-55.

CHAPTER 6

THE MUSAR MOVEMENT AND EMIGRATION

During the short reign of Alexander III (1881-1894), Russian monarchical despotism affirmed itself once again. Alexander's political creed may be reduced to the formula adopted some fifty years earlier by Minister of Education Uvarov: autocracy, orthodoxy and nationalism, with particular emphasis on autocracy.

Autocracy tended to deny popular representation any function in the central government and to impede local self-governmental institutions in exercising their legal rights.

In the matter of orthodoxy, Alexander was a pious man. To him, religion was a matter of personal faith tinged with an element of nationalism. And in the sphere of nationalism, he was influenced by the Pan-Slavs.[1] "I understand only one policy," he said. "[We must extract] from every situation all that is needed by and is useful to Russia, and . . . disregard all other considerations, and . . . act in a straightforward and resolute manner. We can have no policy except one that is purely Russian and national; this is the only policy we can and must follow."[2]

The Influence of Pobedonostsev

Constantine Pobedonostsev (1827-1907), a jurist, was the tutor of Alexander III. From 1880 to 1905 he held the office of chief procurator of the Holy Synod of the Russian Orthodox Church. It was he who molded the mind and character of the Tsar. His correspondence with the Tsar reveals that Alexander eagerly followed his advice in political matters and in appointment-making. The letters of Pobedonostsev were filled with invective against Roman Catholics, Jews, Protestants and Russian dissenters.

---

[1]Pan-Slavism was a movement intended to promote the political and/or cultural unity of all Slavic peoples. In the Russian political spheres of the 1880's and 1890's Pan-Slavism was a means for achievement of Russian aims.

[2]Michael T. Florinsky, *Russia: A History and an Interpretation* (New York, 1964), p. 1088. According to Professor Florinsky, Alexander's application of the principles of orthodoxy and nationalism encouraged administrative centralization and discrimination against religious and ethnic minorities.

Alexander's policies nourished discrimination against and intolerance toward the Jews. "We must not forget," he wrote in a report in 1890 concerning the plight of Russian Jews, "that it was the Jews who crucified our Lord and spilled his precious blood."[3] The prominence of Jews in business and revolutionary movements marked them for attack by revolutionaries and reactionaries.

For example, anti-Semitic forces took advantage of the fact that a Jewish woman, Jessie Helfman, was involved in the assassination of Tsar Alexander II.

The First Pogrom

The first antisemitic outburst in Alexander III's reign took place on April 15, 1881, in Yelisavetgrad (Elizabethgrad), a large city in New Russia with a population of about fifteen thousand Jews. On the eve of the Greek Orthodox Easter the local Christians, gathering in the streets and stores, spoke to one another of the fact that "the Zhyds" (an abusive term for Jews) were about to be beaten. The Jews became frightened. The police, preparing to keep public order during the first of Easter, called out a small brigade of soldiers, and the first days of the holiday passed without incident. On the fourth day (the Greek Orthodox Easter lasts officially three days, but an additional day is celebrated by the people), the troops were taken from the streets, and a pogrom began.

The organizers of the pogrom encouraged a drunken Russian to enter the tavern of a Jew, where he became obnoxious. When the tavernkeeper pushed the troublemaker into the street, the crowd, which was waiting outside, began to shout, "The Jews are beating our people," and to attack Jewish passers-by.

This was the prearranged sign for the riot. Jewish stores were invaded and destroyed, the merchandise looted. At first the police, with the assistance of the troops, managed to scatter the rioters. But on the second day the pogrom was renewed with greater endeavor and better leadership, and the police and the military remained passive.

Committee on Reform

The anti-Jewish outbreaks caused adverse public opinion both at home and abroad. The government decided to initiate reforms.

---

[3]*Ibid.*, p. 1119.

The framing of the new legislation was entrusted to a committee appointed in February, 1883. Count Peter Pahlen, a former minister of justice, presided. The report, which was not made available until 1888, disclosed that discrimination brought nothing but disaster. "The very history of Russian legislation [the report reads] teaches us that there is one way and one solution—the emancipation of the Jews and their assimilation with the rest of the population under the protection of the same laws."[4]

In place of the new restrictions advocated by Pobedonostsev, Pahlen and his committee recommended the gradual abolishment of the prevailing ones. Since the views of the majority of the committee were unacceptable to Alexander III, it was dissolved in 1888 and all its material placed in the archives.[5]

The May Laws

The Temporary Rules of May 3, 1882, subsequently called the May Laws, stated the following provisions:

First, to forbid the Jews to settle anew outside of the towns and townlets.

Second, to suspend the completion of instruments of purchase of real property and merchandise in the name of Jews outside of the towns and townlets.

Third, to forbid the Jews to carry on business on Sundays, and Christian holidays.[6]

The word "temporary" was a trick. Its inclusion made it unnecessary for the orders to obtain the approval of the State Council, where Minister of Interior Nicholas Pavlovich Ignatyev feared opposition. (Temporary orders required only the acquiescence of the Cabinet and the signature of the Tsar.) These orders were never regarded as temporary. Indeed, they remained in effect until the abdication of Tsar Nicholas II in 1917.

The May Laws constituted an economic pogrom against the Jews. The prohibition of business on Sundays and Christian holidays forced a day of idleness upon the poor Jews who had already

---

[4]S. M. Dubnow, *History of the Jews in Russia and Poland*, trans. I. Friedlaender (Philadelphia, 1946), II, 252f.

[5]"Alexander III," *Evreiskaia Enciclopedia*, Vol. I, pp. 825-839, and "Pahlen Commission," pp. 862-863.

[6]S. M. Dubnow, *op. cit.* p. 312.

observed their own Sabbath the day before the Christians'. It also prevented them from doing business with the peasant population which visited the towns on Sundays. The other two measures were intended to make it impossible for Jews to have anything to do with the land or to reside in the arable districts. (Jews were accused of not participating in the agricultural life of the nation, but here the legislative machinery itself was used to deter any Jewish connection with farming.)

There followed other restrictions, namely quotas for Jewish students in secondary schools and higher institutions of learning (1887), and the exclusion of Jews from the legal profession (1889). These restrictions were meant to reduce the number of those "privileged" Jews who, under the law passed in the reign of Alexander II, received as a reward for completing their studies in an institution of higher learning the right to live unhampered throughout the empire. According to S. M. Dubnow, "highly-placed obscurantists contended that the Jewish students exerted an injurious influence upon their Christian comrades from the religious and moral point of view."[7] Pobedonostsev looked upon popular education in general as a harmful force, fraught with danger to monarchical absolutism and the Church. In the words of Dubnow: "There can be but little doubt that the . . . imperial resolutions indicating the necessity of curtailing the number of Jews in the Russian educational establishments were inspired by the 'Grand Inquisitor.' "[8]

The reactionary Minister of Justice, Manassen, was able to persuade the Tsar that it was necessary to check the further admission of Jews to the bar. From a diplomatic point of view, however, it was thought prudent to impose this restriction not as an anti-Jewish ruling but rather as a general decree against all persons of non-Christian persuasion. The restriction was therefore extended to members of the Islam faith and a handful of Karaites.[9]

---

[7]Ibid., p. 348.

[8]Ibid.

[9]The Karaites were a Jewish schismatic sect founded c. 765 in Persia by Anan ben David and originally known as Ananites. Its adherents were called Karaites after the ninth century. The Karaites attacked the Talmudic interpretation of the Bible, rejecting the oral law and interpreting the Bible literally, and they developed their own commentaries, which were in many respects more rigorous and ascetic than the Talmudic interpretations. They produced literature in both Arabic and Hebrew. The sect declined after the twelfth century, but remnants are still extant, notably in Crimea and Israel. *The Columbia Encyclopedia* (New York and London, Third Edition 1963), p. 1113.

In November, 1889, an imperial order decreed the following:

That, pending the enactment of a special law dealing with this subject, the admission of public and private attorneys of non-Christian denominations by the competent judicial institutions and bar associations shall not take place, except with the permission of the Minister of Justice, on the recommendation of the presidents of the above-mentioned institutions and associations.[10]

The Minister of Justice took advantage of the right granted to him of denying admission to Jews as public and private attorneys. (Public attorneys were lawyers of academic standing admitted to the bar by the bar associations. Private attorneys were lawyers without educational qualifications who receive permission from law courts. They are not members of the bar.) The Minister of Justice, "while readily sanctioning the admission of Mohammedans and Karaites . . . almost invariably refused to confirm the election of young Jewish barristers, however warmly they may have been recommended by the judicial institutions and bar associations."[11] From the end of 1889 until 1895, not one single Jewish lawyer received the sanction of the Minister.

The Expulsion of Jews from Moscow

On March 29, 1891, the first day of the Jewish Passover, an alarming whisper ran from mouth to mouth in the synagogues of Moscow, about an imperial decree ordering the expulsion of the Jews from the city and government of Moscow. The order of exile was decreed in two parts on successive days, March 28 and 29. The first part stated that "henceforth no Jewish artisan would be permitted to settle in Moscow."[12] The second part said that "measures would be taken for the gradual removal of the above-mentioned Jews to the Pale."[13] It is hard to imagine that this ukase, with its ambiguous formulation, concealed an order for the uprooting of thousands of Jews.

The first victims were the Jews who lived in Moscow illegally or semi-illegally. Harold Frederic, at that time correspondent in

[10]S. M. Dubnow, *op. cit.*, p. 353.
[11]*Ibid.*
[12]Louis Greenberg, *The Jews in Russia* (New Haven, 1965), II, p. 41.
[13]*Ibid.*

Moscow of the London *Times*, wrote as follows about the raid that took place:

> The whole quarter was ransacked, apartments forced open, doors smashed, every bedroom without exception searched, and every living soul, men, women and children routed out for examination as to their passports. The indignities which the women, young and old alike, underwent at the hands of the Cossacks, may not be described. . . .
> As a result, over 700 men, women and children were dragged at dead of night through the streets to the "out-chastoks" (police stations). They were not even given time to dress themselves, and they were kept in this noisome and overcrowded confinement for thirty-six hours, almost all without food, and some without water as well. Of these unhappy people, thus driven from their beds, and haled off to prison in the wintry darkness, some were afterward marched away by "etape" (that is, chained together with criminals and forced along the roads by Cossacks). A few were bribed out of confinement; the rest were summarily shipped to the Pale. . . . They were chiefly artisans and petty traders. There was no charge of criminality or of leading an evil life against any of them. They were arrested and banished whether their passports were in order or not, and with them, alike to the "outchastoks" and into exile, went their children and womenkind.[14]

The expulsion of about twenty thousand Jews, two-thirds of the Moscow Jewish community, had serious economic consequences for the general population, for the Jews alone employed about twenty-five thousand Russian workmen. Some industries went through grave crises because of the banishment of the Jews and the prohibition against their coming to Moscow even on business. The center of industry shifted from Moscow to Leipzig, Germany. The silk-manufacturing business all but disappeared in Russia. In 1893, representatives from large merchant and manufacturing groups urged in a special memorandum that Jews be permitted to come to

---

[14]Harold Frederic, *The New Exodus: A Study of Israel in Russia* (London, 1892), pp. 287-289.

Moscow for business purposes. The petition was turned down by the police chief.[15]

Emigration

Pogroms and discriminatory legislation resulted, of course, in emigration. The various leaders and spokesmen for the Jewish community had different opinions about this.

An assembly of forty Jewish leaders, including representatives from the Musar Movement, was called under the chairmanship of Baron Horace Gunzburg in St. Petersburg. In April, 1882, a resolution was enacted rejecting completely "the thought of organizing emigration" because it was incompatible with the "historic rights of the Jews to their present fatherland."[16]

Rabbi Israel Salanter favored Jewish emigration to America rather than to Palestine because he felt that Jews would have a better opportunity to earn a living in the New World than in the Holy Land.[17] He was much concerned with the laxity of morality and religious observance in the far distant places of settlement, but he hoped that with economic improvement would come spiritual and moral regeneration.

Other Orthodox Jewish leaders, such as Rabbi Israel Meir Kagan, opposed emigration, because they feared "the ensuing neglect of Jewish rituals and customs among the expatriates in a new and strange world."[18]

Nevertheless, Jewish emigration proceeded apace in ever-increasing numbers.

The best estimates available show that during the entire half century of 1820 to 1870 only some 7,500 Russian and Polish Jews settled in the United States. During the decade of 1871 to 1880 the number of such arrivals suddenly rose over 40,000. It increased again to some 135,000 in the following decade, to grow further to 279,811 from 1891 to 1900 and to 704,245 between 1901 and 1910. It continued at a high rate for four more years until the First World

---

[15]Louis Greenberg, op. cit., p. 44.
[16]Salo W. Baron, The Russian Jew under Tsars and Soviets (New York, 1964), p. 87.
[17]Dov Katz, Tenuath ha-Musar (Tel Aviv, 1952), I, 212ff.
[18]Salo Baron, op. cit., p. 87.

War shut almost all avenues for emigration from Eastern Europe. Needless to say, Jews were not the only ones to leave the Tsarist Empire for the United States. In fact, their ratio among Russian émigrés decreased from decade to decade, and from a majority of 63.3 percent in the 1880's declined to a minority of 44.1 percent between 1901 and 1910.[19]

In addition to the mass emigrations to the United States there were simultaneous emigrations from Russia to Canada (in 1914 the annual peak of 11,252 Eastern European arrivals was reached); South Africa (during 1901 to 1910 there were 17,200 Jewish arrivals alone from Eastern Europe), and other countries in the British Empire. England herself received 120,000 refugees in the four decades before the First World War, despite anti-alien laws which imposed grave restrictions.[20]

In a letter to Pobedonostsev, Russian Jews who emigrated to England wrote the following:

We, the signers of the letter, Russian Jews, who went to England not because of a crime committed against Russia, or because of unwillingness to assume military obligation, or other responsibilities, but because of lack of economic opportunities for a livelihood in the Jewish Pale of Settlement; and the grave poverty forced us to leave the birthplace and to search for a refuge and a livelihood through independent work in a foreign country. Therefore, even now we consider ourselves attached to our birthplace from a moral point of view; the welfare of the birthplace and the will-power to sever the economic, spiritual, and religious life of our brethren in Russia compel us to turn to your honor concerning the Jewish problem, confronting now Russia.[21]

The letter also pointed out that the restrictions against Jews settling in the villages and the denial of permission for Jews to engage in the liquor business would not stop the phantom claim that

---

[19]*Ibid.*, p. 87f.
[20]*Ibid.*, p. 88.
[21]Letter from Russian Jews to Pobedonostsev (London, 1882), *Sichron Jakob*, III, 70-76.

Jews were exploiting the peasants, but would only hurt business, since Russian peasants would no longer be able to sell their farm produce to the Jewish merchants. The Jews in England also urged Pobedonostsev to prevent the issuing of decrees prohibiting teachers from instructing poor Jewish children in traditional Judaism and curtailing the power of rabbis.

Another Assembly in St. Petersburg

In May, 1882, a second assembly gathered in St. Petersburg to discuss the emigrations caused by the discriminatory laws of Alexander III. Rabbis Elijahu Levinsohn, Zev Cohen, Benush Katznelson and others of the Musar Movement participated in the meeting.

"There is merit in emigration," said the majority of the delegates, "but it cannot solve the problem of six million Jews living in Russia; moreover, if the communal leaders continue to occupy themselves with emigration, the anti-Semites will spread the malicious news that the Jews do not love mother Russia and are exploiters of the country; and at a time of distress they are ready to emigrate from the land."[22]

The assembly adopted a resolution calling for lobbying in the higher echelons of the government in order to put an end to the evil talk and discriminations against the Jews. Some lobbyists tried to find favor in the eyes of the Minister of Finance and the Minister of Justice. Others tried to befriend Pobedonostsev, whose influence on the Tsar was well known.

The lobbyists did accomplish this: in 1882 Pobedonostsev wrote, "Behold, I honor and hold in high esteem the ancient people, the Jews, from whom Christianity inherited the fundamentals of her faith, but the young generation of the Jews furthered away from the traditional Judaism of their fathers and followed dangerous paths, which harm even us."[23] The lobbyists were also able to have abolished several laws and decrees injurious to the Jews. Minister of Justice Swilski was heard to say that he himself did not know the value of the discriminatory disabilities against the Jews.

Rabbi Kagan's Concern with the Dispersed

Rabbi Ariah Leib Kagan tells the story of a meeting with his father, Rabbi Israel Meir Kagan, in Warsaw in 1892, in which the

---

[22]*Ibid.* p. 91.
[23]Constantine Pobedonostsev, "The Jews" in *Ha-Meliz* No. 18, 1882.

elder Kagan spoke of his concern over the plight of the Jews in Russia and those who were emigrating to other parts of the world. Rabbi Kagan told his son that mass departure to other countries portended "complete destruction of the Jewish faith and assimilation with the non-Jewish population of [the] new places of settlement."[24] The son answered his father that it would be impossible for him to control the mass emigration because "the majority of the emigrants [had] no place to settle due to the banishment from the villages and Moscow by Alexander III."[25] Rabbi Ariah Kagan advised his father as follows:

> If you are zealous of the honor of God and His Torah, you must follow the emigrants and also settle in America, and in America travel from city to city and persuade them in the morning and in the evening to follow the teachings of the Torah, also to establish large gatherings to strengthen Torah and observance, and I [bring] proof from the Prophet Jeremiah who rebuked the Jews for departing to Egypt but we read afterward that he also followed the Jews to Egypt and he preached the words of God to the Jews of Egypt.[26]

The father was impressed by the advice of his son but did not answer him. Half a year went by, and then the son received a manuscript dealing with rules for emigrants. The manuscript was published in 1893 and was called *Nidhei Israel* (*The Dispersed of Israel*).

Rabbi Israel Meir Kagan of the Musar Movement did not depart for America. However, his book was an excellent substitute for his presence. Jews in America, England, Africa and elsewhere made time to study the laws dealing with the problems of the dispersed. The book was translated into Yiddish, so that women and laymen would be able to learn from it.

The title of the book, *Nidhei Israel*, comes from the following verse: "If any of thine that are dispersed be in the uttermost parts of heaven from thence will the Lord thy God gather thee." (Deuteronomy 30.4) Rabbi Kagan felt this way:

---

[24]Rabbi Israel Meir Kagan, *Michtavei Hafets Hayyim* (New York, 1953), p. 55.
[25]*Ibid.*
[26]*Ibid.*

"And, behold, when we discern now the keeping of the precepts of the Torah and its statutes in this world, indeed, it is very lax, even for those people living unpersecuted at home, and especially for people wandering in the distant lands, like America, Africa, and England."[27]

According to Rabbi Kagan, laxity in observing the precepts of the Torah can occur in four ways.

For instance, a new immigrant may attribute transgressions of the precepts of the Torah to the problems of adjustment to life in the new country. He reasons that his wanderings are a punishment from God, therefore it is logical to assume that God has forsaken him.

The above conclusion results in despair in observance of the law of God and, at times, violation of the most significant laws, such as Sabbath observance and sex rules, and anarchy becomes the guide to the Torah.[28]

A second cause of laxity in observance is ignorance—lack of knowledge regarding the conduct of oneself according to the laws of the Torah. The lack of education in the basic laws and the want of personnel dedicated to strengthening faith in God and Torah cause people to depart from religious ways. Shame, which prevented such departures in the old country, is usually absent in the new lands of refuge, and this lack of shame leads people astray.[29]

The most important cause of laxity is the newcomer's discovery that his acquaintances from the old country look disdainfully upon religious practice in the new country. The new immigrant feels that, after all, he is not alone in this matter; as it is with the rest of the people in town, so will it be with him.[30]

A final cause of laxity is the neglect of the study of Torah, which eventually leads to the destruction of religion.[31]

The book *Nidhei Israel* showed great understanding of the religious, social, cultural and economic problems of the Jews in distant lands as well as of those in the old country. It found a market in America, Africa, and Canada, not to mention the success it made in Europe. A rabbi from America, visiting Rabbi Kagan, informed

---

[27]Rabbi Israel Meir Kagan, *Nidhei Israel* (Warsaw, 1893), p. 22f.
[28]*Ibid.*
[29]*Ibid.*, p. 23f.
[30]*Ibid.*, p. 24.
[31]*Ibid.*, p. 78.

him that the religious life of the Jews there was improving from day to day.

Rabbi Ariah Kagan wrote:

> The great utility this work brought to thousands of our brethren in the lands of their dispersal is not to be related or evaluated. It saved them from assimilation among the nations and withdrawal from the root of hoary Israel, and who can measure the greatness of the need for the book at this time, when the religion has been so very fearfully thrown down. The foundations of the Torah, like Sabbath keeping, Kashruth, purity of family life, phylacteries, and more are almost completely forgotten.[32]

Rabbi Jacob Joseph

In 1886, the Jewish community of New York appealed to the outstanding rabbis of Europe for a chief rabbi of New York Jewry. Rabbi Jacob Joseph, a follower of the Musar Movement, was appointed Chief Rabbi of the largest Jewish settlement in the New World. His mission was to raise the low status of traditional Judaism and to help the immigrants to adjust to the new environment without abandoning religious practice.

Rabbi Joseph started to work immediately to improve religious life, but unfortunately he was not too successful. Nevertheless, he was active in establishing the rabbinical seminary Etz Haim, the forerunner of Yeshiva University's Isaac Elhanan Theological Seminary. He also endorsed strict supervision in kashruth in the slaughterhouses of New York.

Rabbi Joseph was the first and last chief rabbi in New York. The lure of the secular society and the temptations to the new immigrants to make more and more money rendered him ineffectual in influencing them to remain observant.

---

[32]See Rabbi Ariah Leib Kagan's foreword to *The Dispersed of Israel* (trans. New York, 1951), p. xx.

CHAPTER 7

THE MUSAR MOVEMENT AND ERETZ ISRAEL

In order to understand the Musar Movement's attitude toward Zionism and the Jewish settlement in Israel, it is important to trace some historical aspects of the Hobebe Zion (Lovers of Zion) and Zionist movements, for these came to have a direct influence upon the Musar Movement's reactions toward these settlements in Israel (then Palestine, and thus referred to herein) from 1890 onward.

Throughout the nineteenth century Palestine[1] was in a state of neglect. Vegetation and soil conservation were disregarded by the inhabitants. The roads were dangerous and sometimes impassable. Epidemics, crop failure, and earthquakes brought about disease and starvation, and a scarcity of water was the order of the day.

In 1841 Palestine had been assigned to the Ottoman Empire by the European powers, who began to take some interest in the country. Church missions went there, and consulates were set up for their protection. This protection worked to the advantage of the Jews also, who flocked into the country and put themselves under the sovereignty of the various European powers.[2]

In his first visit to Jerusalem in 1827 Sir Moses Montefiore[3] found fewer than a thousand persons in the city. On his seventh visit, in 1875, the Jewish population was estimated in excess of 12,000, increasing to 35,000 by 1885.[4] In the early nineteenth century Sephardic Jews from Levantine countries settled in Palestine and constituted the majority of the Jewish Population. The Se-

---

[1]Edward Robinson, *Biblical Researches in Palestine*, II, 81; III, 30, on Palestine a hundred years ago.

[2]Ismar Elbogen, *A Century of Jewish Life* (Philadelphia, 1960), p. 245.

[3]Sir Moses Haim Montefiore (1784-1885), British-Jewish philanthropist, was affiliated with the Rothschilds and retired in 1821 from business to devote himself to philanthropy and to securing political and civil emancipation for Jews in England. As president of the Board of Deputies of British Jews he worked to alleviate discriminatory practices against Jews in Europe and the Near East. He founded a hospital and girls' school in Jerusalem in 1855 and was influential in stimulating the rise of Jewish nationalism, out of which developed modern political Zionism. *The Columbia Encyclopedia*, Third Edition (New York and London, 1963).

[4]Ismar Elbogen, *op. cit.*

89

phardic Jews are of Spanish and Portuguese origin. Their customs, rituals, synagogue services, and Hebrew pronunciation differ from those of the Ashkenazim. The name Ashkenazim applied to the Jews of Germany and North France from the tenth century on. In the middle of the sixteenth century, the term came to include the Jews of Eastern Europe. The pogroms and discriminations against the Jews by Alexander III caused Ashkenazic Jews to emigrate to Palestine in the second half of the nineteenth century and to become the majority. The hardships they faced were no different from those confronted earlier by Sephardic Jews.

> The pioneer colonists in the ancient fatherland met with enormous obstacles in their path; the opposition of the Turkish Government which hindered in every possible way the purchase of land and acquisition of property; the neglected condition of the soil, the uncivilized state of neighboring Arabs, the lack of financial means and of agricultural experience.[5]

In spite of these problems, in 1882, the first year of the Hobebe Zion movement, the settlement of Rishon le-Zion, near Jaffa, became a reality.[6] Subsequently a few more settlements arose: Ekron and Ghederah, Yesod Hamaalah, Rosh-Pinah, and Zikron Yacob in the Galilee. Rabbi Ariah Leib Kagan wrote:

> I remember that in 1890 and in 1891, when they began to expel our brothers from Moscow, there emerged a big movemen to our holy land. Hundreds and thousands of the evicted Jews hastened to take refuge in the land of our fathers. They bought there land; they planted vineyards; they established colonies; inside the colony they congregated at meetings; they set up societies; they sent representatives to purchase land. Property-owners sold their homes and possessions; and with the money they settled with joy in Palestine. They were looking hopefully to find happiness and prosperity there.[7]

---

[5]S. M. Dubnow, *History of the Jews in Russia and Poland*, trans. by I. Friedlaender (Philadelphia, 1946), II, 375.
[6]*Ibid.*
[7]Ariah Leib Kagan, *Michtavei Hafets Hayyim* (New York, 1953), p. 43.

The Hobebe Zion in Russia were able to attract the support of the prominent Rabbi Samuel Mohilever (1824-1898) [8] of Bialystok. His affiliation with the Hobebe Zion was "largely instrumental in weakening the opposition of the Orthodox masses which were inclined to look upon this political movement as a rival of the traditional Messianic ideas of Judaism."[9]

At the same time, Moses Lilienblum (1843-1910) and Dr. Leo Pinsker (1821-1891) organized Hobebe Zion societies in Odessa and other Russian cities. Toward the end of 1884 the delegates of these societies came together at a conference in the Prussian border town of Kattowitz. (It would have been impossible to hold the conference in Russia because of the danger of police interference.) At the conference a fund, "Mazkeret Moshe" (A Memorial to Moses), was established, in honor of Sir Moses Montefiiore, whose hundredth birthday was celebrated that year. Hobebe Zion centers in Odessa and Warsaw collected money for supporting the Jewish settlements in Palestine.

Rabbi Kagan's Reaction to Hobebe Zion and Jewish Settlement

The reaction of Rabbi Israel Meir Kagan to the Jewish settlements in Palestine and to the Hobebe Zion movement in Russia is described by his son:

> I received a letter from my father. . . . In it he informs me about the immense movement among our people in every corner of the country to settle in Palestine; and he calculates that the days are days of the coming of the Messiah; and since God remembered his people, perhaps it is the beginning of the gathering of the dispersed Jews that takes place before the coming of the Messiah; and if we had the means we would buy land and settle in Palestine. Since we do not have the means to settle in Palestine, let us do what is within our reach. Behold, if God shall return his exiled people to our land, are we not obligated to build the Temple and the altar, and to bring sacrifices?[10]

[8]Nahum Sokolow, *History of Zionism 1600-1918*, with an introduction by A. J. Balfour (London, 1919), II, 289f.

[9]S. M. Dubnow, *op. cit.*, p. 377.

[10]See *Michtavei Hafets Hayyim, op. cit.*, p. 436.

Rabbi Salanter's Disciples' Settlement in Palestine

When the Zionists established the bank for colonization in Palestine, Rabbi Isaac Blazer said he considered the enterprise heaven-inspired, but was "surprised that the religious Jews who pray for Zion several times a day did not think of the idea which was germinated by non-religious Zionists."[11]

A lover of Palestine since his youth, Rabbi Blazer had always longed to dwell in the Holy Land. In 1901 the board of directors of the rabbinical seminary Or Hadas (New Light) requested him to come to Jerusalem, and he accepted the offer. On his way there he thanked God that he and his family were to see the land "that Moses and Aaron were not fortunate to witness in person."[12]

He arrived in Jaffa in 1904. Rabbi Abraham Isaac Kook and leading rabbis of Jerusalem received him with great warmth. He bought a home in Jerusalem and immediately began actively contributing to the religious life of the new land. He became dean of the post-graduate Rabbinical Seminary of Vilna and Zamuth in Jerusalem. In addition, he served as chairman of the board of directors and as dean of Or Israel. He participated in the city affairs of Jerusalem as a member of the Jerusalem Rabbinate. His influence in strengthening the spiritual and moral life of the Jews in Palestine was substantial.[13]

A month before the high holy days Rabbi Blazer lectured on morality and piety to huge crowds in Jerusalem. His dynamic personality and persuasive ability motivated many to follow the teachings of the Musar Movement.

In 1906 Rabbi Naphtali Amsterdam, a disciple of Rabbi Salanter and a close friend of Rabbi Blazer, came to live in the Holy Land. In Jerusalem he set up a class for the study of morality and he also taught musar to the laymen. An ardent worker in communal matters, he is best known for the establishment of an old-age home in Jerusalem known as Osef Nidahim (Gathering of the Dispersed.) [14]

---

[11]Dov Katz, *Tenuath ha-Musar* (Tel Aviv, 1954), II, 253. It was told by Rabbi Simon Hurwitz in the name of Rabbi Blazer.

[12]Letter of Rabbi Joseph Hayyim Sonnenfeld, 4th day of Adar, 1901, in Dov Katz, *Ibid.*, p. 254.

[13]This is based on the correspondence between Rabbi Blazer and Rabbi Naphtali Amsterdam, Dov Katz, *Ibid.*, p. 254.

[14]Based on a letter from Rabbi Abraham Kook to Rabbi Naphtali Amsterdam, praising him for his work in behalf of the aged, Dov Katz, *Ibid.*, p. 284.

Rabbi Elijahu Levensohn, the eminent lobbyist and prominent disciple of Rabbi Salanter, worked arduously to raise money for the Jewish settlement in Palestine. For forty years he headed the financial department of the post-graduate Rabbinical Seminary of Vilna and Zamuth in Jerusalem.

Rabbi Eliezer Sulbitz settled in Palestine in 1923. He set up a branch of the Rabbinical Seminary of Lomza, Poland in Petach Tikva, Palestine. His son-in-law, Rabbi Yehiel Mordecai Gordon, was sent to America to raise funds for building this seminary and for bringing students from Europe to Petach Tikva. The Lomza seminary fell victim to Nazi persecutions. The students who managed to survive went to Petach Tikva after the second World War.

Rabbi Isaac Meltzen, a follower of the Musar Movement, challenged the secular Zionism of Theodor Herzl, Nahum Sokolow, and others. He believed that redemption would come "through a miracle and not through natural phenomena," and that God did not need the help of man.[15] Despite his criticism of secular Zionism, however, Rabbi Meltzen loved and longed for the Holy Land. He liked Hebrew and tried to use it in his home. In 1906, he left Russia and was appointed chief examiner of students at the rabbinical seminary Or Israel. He set up groups to study morality and lectured to the masses on the same subject.

Rabbi Zvi Levitan settled in Jerusalem in 1902 and founded several institutions for Torah and moral learning. He helped to build the famous synagogue in Givat Saul. He arranged lessons in Torah and morality for the workers. Rabbi Levitan was very much interested in the Sephardic Jews in Palestine and set up study groups for them. A month before the high holy days he preached repentance every Sabbath to large crowds.

Emigration from Lithuania

Emigration to Palestine gained momentum in the 1920's, prompting rabbinical students from Lithuania to settle in the Holy Land. In 1924 a part of the famous Slobodca Yeshiva, under the leadership of Rabbi Nathan Zvi Finkel and Rabbi Moses Mordecai, emigrated to Palestine.

Rabbinical students in Lithuania were as a rule exempt from

---

[15]See Dov Katz, *Ibid.*, p. 392.

military conscription. However, as the Lithuanian government began to pass restrictions on the Jews, the law requiring rabbinical seminaries to institute in the high school curriculum the study of the Lithuanian language and secular subjects in order for the students to be exempted from military duty was very disturbing to deans and students alike. On the one hand, the Rabbinical Seminary of Telshe decided to accept the decree of the government and set up a curriculum in the high school for the study of the Lithuanian language and secular subjects. On the other hand, Rabbi Finkel, at the Slobodca Yeshiva, refused to execute the decree of the government lest secular studies be harmful to the moral and spiritual life of the students.

And so in the summer of 1924 a large number of Slobodca students had to report for the draft. The conscription threatened the very existence of the Slobodca Yeshiva. Rabbi Finkel, concerned about the problems of religious Jewish soldiers in the army, encouraged his students to emigrate.

In fact, in light of the situation confronting the Slobodca students, the leaders of the seminary decided to transplant part of the seminary to Israel immediately.[16] Rabbi Finkel had wanted to settle in the Holy Land with his students before the First World War. In 1913, when Rabbi Jacob David and his son-in-law, Rabbi Joseph Knovitz, a student of Rabbi Finkel, settled in Palestine in Sefat, Rabbi Finkel had made plans to establish, under their supervision, a rabbinical seminary in Sefat. However, with the outbreak of the the First World War, his plans had not materialized.

Establishment of the Hebron Yeshiva

The ancient city of Hebron was selected as the site for the Palestine branch of the Slobodca Yeshiva. Rabbi Moses Mordecai, who was in America to raise funds for the Slobodca Yeshiva in Europe, undertook the responsibility of raising money for the new branch. He organized a group of donors each of whom contributed a thousand dollars. Twenty-five thousand dollars was raised without difficulty in America. In addition, the twenty-five contributors agreed to set up a permanent committee to help in the future to support the Palestine branch of the Slobodca Yeshiva.

---

[16]Dov Katz, *Tenuath ha-Musar* (Tel Aviv, 1954), III, p. 88. Dov Katz is a primary source for study of Slobodca. He studied in Slobodca and settled in Israel.

Rabbi Yehezkiel Sarna was appointed to go to Palestine to find the location for the new seminary. With the help of Rabbi Haim Berlin, president of the Mizrachi organization and a member of the Zionist leadership, permission was obtained to establish the seminary in Hebron.

Hebron was the home and burial place of the Jewish ancestors. It had also been a serene location from the political point of view; however, it was fast becoming a cause of quarrel between Jews and Arabs in other parts of Palestine. Jewish leaders in Palestine saw, in choosing Hebron for the Yeshiva, a great opportunity for attracting Jewish settlers in an area which was predominantly Arab.

The Hebron Yeshiva was the first one in the Holy Land to emulate the style of learning, the stress of morality, and the piety of the Musar seminaries of Lithuania.[17]

In 1924, ten students came from Europe to study at the Hebron Yeshiva. The seminary was officially opened. In 1925, a hundred students were selected by the Slobodca Yeshiva to study at Hebron. Students from Poland, Lithuania, and other countries emigrated to Palestine to study Torah and morality at the Hebron Yeshiva.

The Hebron Yeshiva was a phenomenon in Jewish history. For the first time, one hundred students, along with other outstanding scholars, uprooted themselves from established schools in other countries to come to the Holy Land.[18] Jews all over the world were inspired by this example and hoped that Palestine would again become the center for learning, spiritual life, and morality. Other European seminaries attempted to open branches in Palestine. Even the British High Commissioner in Palestine mentioned the establishment of the yeshiva in Hebron as an event of paramount importance.[19]

Rabbi Sarna assumed the educational and managerial responsibilities of the yeshiva. He was assisted by Rabbi Abraham Grodzenski, who came from Europe. Under their leadership, the Hebron Yeshiva won acclaim as an outstanding seminary for learning, spiritual life, and morality. Rabbi Moses Mordecai, whose fund-raising accomplishments had made all of this possible, arrived in 1925 to observe the fruits of his labor.

---

[17]*Ibid.*, p. 90.
[18]*Ibid.*
[19]*Ibid.*

Rabbi Finkel Arrives in Hebron

In July, 1925, Rabbi Finkel arrived in Hebron. He was an old man at the time and was to lose his son in the following year, but despite this he displayed remarkable energy, and was able to provide leadership in Hebron. He manifested a great love for the Holy Land and inspired his students with this love.

For example, in his early weeks in Hebron Rabbi Finkel went for a walk and saw rocks in the road. He picked them up and put them aside. His students thought he removed the rocks in order to prevent an accident; however, he told them that rocks on the road could bring the Holy Land a bad reputation, and his love for the land forced him to keep the roads clear.[20] His visits to holy places inspired others to feel that even the rocks were sanctified, that the land of Jerusalem, the stones, and the sand of the holy city were filled with holiness.

Under Rabbi Finkel's leadership the Hebron Yeshiva flourished. Entrance was sought by students throughout the world. Rabbi Finkel's students were always welcomed in his home, and Sabbath eves were filled with spiritual and moral inspiration. Religious and non-religious Zionists alike in the Jewish settlement in Palestine admired the high learning, spiritual life and morality of the students at the Hebron Yeshiva.[21] Sons of old settlers in Palestine were happy to educate their sons in Hebron.

Many Jews began to settle in Hebron. Tourism from abroad began to climb. In the areas around Hebron new settlements were founded by Jews. In Migdal Eter, on the way from Jerusalem to Hebron, a religious Kibbutz (collective settlement) was established. The Arabs in Hebron sold their homes to Jews in the vicinity of the yeshiva, so that the students might have a place to live.

Schools Elsewhere in Palestine

In the city of Haifa, Rabbi Finkel helped to set up the day school Tifereth Israel, for adolescents. In Tel Aviv, he was active in establishing a post-graduate seminary for married students. He appointed Rabbi Samuel Funtiler, from Europe, to head this institution, hoping to make it a center for spreading Torah and morality throughout the Jewish settlement in Palestine. Rabbi Funtiler

---

[20]Told by Rabbi Ephraim Sokolover in Dov Katz, *Ibid.*, III, p. 93f.
[21]*Ibid.*, p. 97.

failed in this function. However, Rabbi Finkel's students were successful, in 1931, in injecting new life into the idea, and the seminary at Tel Aviv was named Hechal ha-Talmud. This was the first institution of higher learning in Tel Aviv and its environs to inaugurate a program of Torah and moral learning, and it produced outstanding rabbis and teachers.

Rabbi Finkel continued to take an interest in the management of the Slobodca Yeshiva, thus contributing to Torah learning, spiritual life, and morality in Slobodca as well as in the Holy Land.

Secularism of Hobebe Zion

Rabbi Israel Meir Kagan and other religious Jews were perturbed by the fact that the leadership of the Hobebe Zion was being taken over by followers of the Enlightenment. They recalled that teachers of Hobebe Zion leaders "erased from the Prayer Book all the blessings that make mention of the name of our land."[22] Now, the Maskilim were gathering money for the colonies in Palestine, and were setting up Hobebe Zion associations in Russia.

Rabbi Kagan did not have confidence in the attempts of the men of the Enlightenment to return the Jews to the Holy Land. In his words: "Can from such people thrust forth an iota of goodness? Can such people merit the Divine Presence to guide their deeds? And if God will not construct the Temple, in vain labored its builders. If they examine the nature of the members of the Hobebe Zion center in Odessa, Russia, their majority's spiritual value is foreign to the religion of Israel."[23]

One of the mainstays of Odessa's center was perhaps the most distinguished of the group. "He did not even know our holy tongue (even though his father was one of the greatest enlighteners in the generation before ours, and published books in our tongue, despite this he did not find it necessary to teach his son as part of the other studies our holy language and our Prayer Book)."[24] Dr. Leo Pinsker is the man who fits the description of the quotation, because he did not know Hebrew. He was the son of Simhah Pinsker (1801-1864), a Hebrew grammarian and the author of several books, and he was also one of the leaders of the Hobebe Zion movement in Odessa.

---

[22]See *Michtavei Hafets Hayyim, op. cit.,* p. 69.
[23]*Ibid.,* p. 70.
[24]*Ibid.*

Rabbi Kagan and the other religious Jews were upset with certain members of the Odessa Hobebe Zion, because "they were known throughout our people as disbelievers in the teachings of the Torah, as publishers of sharp articles against the Mishnah and the Talmud, as critics of the Torah . . . and as persuaders of the young generation caused the youth to deny everything which has to do with holiness."[25]

The leader of the Odessa group could be no other than Moses Lilienblum. To him, the teachings of the Talmud were nothing but superstition, and his early education a "sin against youth." Another victim of the anger of the rabbis was Perez Smolenskin (1842-1885). From the pages of the literary periodical *Ha-Shahar* he battled the rabbis. However, after the persecutions and massive emigrations of the Jews both Lilienblum and Smolenskin came back—not to traditional Judaism, but to Jewish nationalism.

Rabbi Kagan received letters from other rabbis complaining that Jews in Palestine who were assisted financially and morally by the Hobebe Zion were not keeping the precepts of the Torah. The leaders of Hobebe Zion were guilty, they said, not only of "leading astray the Jews in the Diaspora, but also [of wanting] to promulgate their ideas and abominations in the only remaining place of refuge, that is the holy place of all Jews."[26]

Rabbi Ariah Leib Kagan wrote as follows about Theodor Herzl and the rise of Zionism:

> The religious Jews fomented the most commotion at the time of the emergence on the platform in behalf of our people of Theodor Herzl and his friends, who came from long assimilated families; there were certain members who had non-Jewish wives. Herzl and his friends called for congresses; and there they enacted statutes for the land of Palestine; and there irreligiosity was explicitly expressed; and one has no right to question a person's religion and his belief; and no man should be deprived of his part in behalf of Zionism because of his relationship to the Creator.[27]

[25] *Ibid.*
[26] *Ibid.*
[27] *Ibid.* p. 71.

Many discussions regarding culture took place in Zionist congresses. Schools were established in Jaffa, where children were indoctrinated in heresy through the Biblical criticism of German scholars, who "degrad[ed] the Holy Books to dust."[28]

Religious Jews criticized the followers of the Enlightenment for sending speakers to different cities to arouse Jews to contribute money for the building of the Holy Land. They felt in particular that the Maskilim were mocking the faith in the Messianic coming—a faith that had given Jews the strength to withstand persecution throughout the generations. Religious Jews felt that the followers of the Enlightenment exchanged Messianic days for the motto of "possessing some land in Palestine." Rabbi Ariah Leib Kagan wrote: "How stupid are these enlighteners. Instead of capturing the heart of the people and strengthening their hearts that the Messianic days are near and the beginning of the dispersed of Israel is taking place already, they use the land possession motto."[29]

If the leaders of the Zionist movement had taken a religious tone, if they had talked of rebuilding the Temple and Jerusalem, religious Jews would have supported the State of Israel. In other words, religious Jews did not object to Zionism and to a Jewish state in Palestine, but they did despise Zionism's lack of religiousness. The Maskilim with their irreligious speeches alienated traditional Jews, who were deeply hurt by the denial that God would have a hand in the rebuilding of the Holy Land. The followers of the Enlightenment disregarded the sages of their generation. They did not permit the rabbis to "mix in" on the issue of Palestine. And the "enlightened" Jews called the rabbis "rebels of the Enlightenment who grow wise by exploiting the poor."[30]

The religious Jews were wounded because they longed to touch the earth of the Holy Land, and the Zionist movement with its secular nationalism prevented them from participating in the rebuilding of Palestine. Pious Jews were confronted with the dilemma of the interpretation of the Zionist movement: since Zionism denies the coming of the Messiah, God wants to try the faith of His followers. The Zionist leaders and the movement do not act according to the Torah; therefore, who is responsible for the Zionist

---

[28]*Ibid.*, p. 72.
[29]*Ibid.*
[30]*Ibid.*, p. 73.

movement, God or Satan? This burning question about God's hand or Satan's hand in the emergence of the Zionist movement caused unrest among the religious Jews.[31]

Rabbi Israel Meir Kagan received protests from many rabbis concerning his silence and lack of objection against the leaders of the Zionist movement as well as against the mocking of religion. By nature Rabbi Kagan was a man who avoided quarrels, and in the dispute over the Zionist movement he tried to avert further altercation. Nevertheless, "his heart was broken upon hearing that the leaders of Zionism [were] leading Jews astray in the colonies in Palestine and at home from the ways of the Torah; he revealed his mind only to his close friends and to the friends of rabbinical seminaries."[32]

Soon, however, his stand on the irreligiosity of Zionism was announced among the religious Jews. Zionist leaders, who were anxious to receive the support of the most illustrious rabbi of his day, argued with Rabbi Kagan about his acceptance of "false information" about the heresy in the colonies in Palestine. Rabbi Kagan's stand was this:

He denied "young scholarly-religious students under his jurisdiction [permission] to follow in the footsteps of the irreligious Zionist leaders, especially when one of the enlightened Zionists, reputed for always telling the truth, after his visiting all the schools in Palestine, testified that in the schools the critical method [was] used to study the Holy Books."[33] The enlightened Zionist reputed for his candor was Asher Ginzberg, the eminent antagonist of political Zionism as the solution to Jewish problems.

Asher Ginzberg (1856-1927), also known by his pen name Ahad Ha-am (One of the People), was from the beginning a critic of political Zionism. Nor was he pleased with the Eastern European form of Zionism which stressed economic remedy. His Zionism was positive and spiritual. Material things were secondary to him. He felt that the Palestine settlement should try to exploit the scattered energies of the Jews, and should serve as an example of Jews everywhere for cultural and spiritual regeneration.

The followers of the Enlightenment published hundreds of

[31]*Ibid.*
[32]*Ibid.*
[33]*Ibid.*

articles concerning Jewish nationalism, all stressing the following idea: "A nation is composed of the language and the land, and without them it is not called a nation." "Therefore," wrote Rabbi Ariah Leib Kagan, "they urged the people to build the land and correct the language. When one of the Maskilim wrote an article in the periodical "Ha-Meliz" that it is possible to be called a Jew without the keeping of the Torah, then my father could not keep silent any longer."[34]

The response of Rabbi Israel Meir Kagan was swift: "Our nation exists only because of the keeping of the Torah and the precepts, and not because of the land and the language. If we do not heed the precepts of God, the land and the language will not save us. Our fathers were already there, and because they sinned they were exiled from the Holy Land."[35]

Rabbi Kagan's statement spread to religious and non-religious Jews. Persons of both persuasions knew that he "was not one of the extremist Orthodox Jews opposing Zionism; he did not request from the pioneers that they should be engrossed all their days in the study of Torah and prayer; but only [that] they shall comport themselves according to the precepts of the Torah, as [do] all observant Jews in exile."[36]

In 1927, Rabbi Kagan wrote the following in a letter:
All the Jews believe in the coming of the Messiah and [that] Elijah will come and bring good tidings to us before his coming; and in every prayer we recite to God that He shall dispatch to us our righteous Messiah, and He shall construct the Temple as soon as possible in our days . . . therefore, we are obligated to prepare ourselves in the study of the Temple and sacrifices in order to merit without ignorance the Messiah.[37]

All his life Rabbi Kagan had longed to settle in Palestine, and in 1928 he made preparations to do so. When his plans became public, a committee of leading rabbis and deans of theological seminaries requested him to postpone his journey, because the sem-

[34]Ibid., p. 74.
[35]Ibid.
[36]Ibid., p. 76.
[37]Letter from Rabbi Israel Meir Kagan, Radun, Poland, ADAR Bet, 1927, in Michtavei Hafets Hayyim, op. cit., p. 21-23.

inaries needed his guidance in the critical time of their existence. Rabbi Kagan complied, and in 1933 he died, at the age of ninety-five, without having fulfilled his dream of seeing Palestine.

Rabbi Kagan's view on Israel can be summarized by the following statement: "The soul of Israel is the sacred Torah; and the body of Israel is the land of Israel. Surely the soul cannot exist without the body; and all the precepts of the Torah depending on the land for their fulfillment cannot be carried out without the land of Israel."[38]

He felt that there was no future for Jews in exile; in one place it was forbidden for Jews to dwell, in another the Jews were persecuted, in a third they were prohibited from trading and from owning property. "Despite all the hardships in the exile, the Jewish people exist; but the land of Palestine without Torah, behold, is a measure of land; it is a body without a soul; and goodness is the result of the amalgamation of Torah and the land of Israel."[39]

One of his students, Rabbi Moses M. Yosher, wrote the following:

> In the radiance of his faith there was no shadow of doubt. He looked confidently to the fulfillment of the Divine promise. . . . He prayed for Israel's total rehabilitation, not a homeland in reduced territory or mere political independence. It was not worthwhile, he said, to become another Albania or even another Belgium after nineteen centuries of suffering. A state must be a reign of justice and godliness, with holy Temple restored and sacrificial offerings reinstated.[40]

[38]Rabbi Israel Meir Kagan, *Hafets Hayyim al Ha-Torah*, ed., Rabbi Samuel Greiniman (Bnei Brak, Israel), p. 99.

[39]*Ibid.*

[40]Rabbi Moses M. Yosher, "Israel Meir he-Kohen—Hafets Hayyim," *Jewish Leaders*, ed. Rabbi Leo Jung (Jerusalem, 1953), p. 468f.

CHAPTER 8

THE MUSAR MOVEMENT'S PARTICIPATION
IN COMMUNAL PROBLEMS

Rabbi Salanter's Participation in Vilna

In 1848, cholera spread throughout the city of Vilna, causing many deaths. Rabbi Salanter assisted in caring for the sick. Rabbi Salanter was convinced that every Jew, particularly men of the Talmud, were obligated to help the sick. He therefore assumed the leadership in Vilna in setting up relief works. He rented, at great expense, a hospital of five hundred beds. Under his influence, doctors worked without pay and a group of seventy men gathered to help in the emergency. Rabbi Salanter permitted Jews to do all necessary work on the Sabbath to care for the sick.

He commanded the people to heed the advice of the doctors. He made a proclamation that eating fish which was prohibited during the epidemic was like eating pork. He advised the Jews not to fear, not to worry, not to mourn too long—because this caused physical exhaustion, which in turn led to cholera.[1]

On Yom Kippur, the Day of Atonement, during the plague, Rabbi Salanter told the Jews not to fast but to have food and water. Other rabbis would not come out in the open with the statement that food was permissible on the Day of Atonement during the cholera epidemic.

After the morning service was completed on the Day of Atonement, Rabbi Salanter "ascended the platform and recited a blessing over cookies and wine before everybody because he feared lest the people heed not his proclamation of eating on the Day of Atonement."[2] This incident created a stir among many of the rabbis, who felt that Israel Salanter, who was young and without a pulpit, had no right to make such a proclamation to the public.[3]

---

[1]Letter from Rabbi Salanter to a colleague stating his views on what was permitted and what was prohibited during the plague, in Isaac Blazer, *Or Israel* (Vilna, 1900), p. 67.

[2]Dov Katz, *Tenuath ha-Musar* (Tel Aviv, 1952), I, 160. See also Maggid Steinschneider, *Ir Vilna* (Vilna, 1900), p. 130, and Baruch Epstein, *Makor Baruch* (Vilna, 1928), II, p. 1012.

[3]Told by T. Weinberg, *op. cit.*, p. 161.

But Rabbi Salanter did more than this. He announced that he would deliver a lecture of rabbinic law in the Big Synagogue of Vilna. The rabbis of the city, thinking that he was going to discuss the laws of not fasting on the Day of Atonement, gathered to hear him. Then he surprised everyone by avoiding discussion of this issue. Instead, he discussed other topics "with brilliant dialectics, deep understanding and sharpness of mind."[4] He displayed his knowledge to win recognition, in order to save lives.[5] The rabbis of Vilna realized that he was an authority on every aspect of rabbinic law. His name and word of his noble deeds spread throughout Russia, winning him respect for his courage and determination to help others.

Rabbi Salanter in Kovna

Many well-known Talmudists in the vicinity of Kovna attended Rabbi Salanter's discourses on Torah and morality. At the same time, Rabbi Salanter did not neglect the masses, to whom he spoke with simplicity and warmth.

Rabbi Israel Salanter took an active interest in teaching Torah and morality to college-educated Jews. He sent one of his best students, Israel Iser Einhorn, to the Petersburg Institute of Military Medicine. Einhorn became a high-ranking doctor in the Russian army. Unfortunately, as time passed, he became converted to the Russian Orthodox faith, causing great grief to Rabbi Salanter. However, Einhorn's younger brother also became a doctor in the army—but remained committed to the commands of Judaism, thus setting an example to other Jews.[6] In almost all of the cities of Lithuania Rabbi Salanter encouraged workingmen to form groups to study law and ethics, using the books *Chai Adam* (*Life of Man*) and *Msilath Yesarim* (*Path of the Righteous*).[7] Many men made progress with these books and were also enthusiastic in their study of *Ein Jacob* (*Eye of Jacob*) and the Mishnah.[8]

In teaching the book *Chai Adam*, Rabbi Salanter's purpose was not only to relate the laws to the masses, but also to train them

---

[4]*Ibid.*

[5]*Ibid.*

[6]*Ibid.*, p. 178. See also E. E. Freedman, *Sefer ha-Zichronoth* (Tel Aviv, 1926), p. 79.

[7]Told in *Ha-Meliz*, Adar 1st, 1883, in Dov Katz, *op. cit.*, p. 179.

[8]Based on the archives of Dr. N. Eherman.

to study the laws by themselves. He urged teachers to explain every word in the beginning of the lesson and afterwards to repeat the whole sentence; and the listeners were to repeat everything several times to their teachers.[9]

Rabbi Salanter in Germany

After nine successful years in Kovna, Rabbi Salanter went to Germany, where Reform Judaism, secular education and assimilation were active forces among the Jews. Many Russian Jews were startled by his departure for Germany, but Rabbi Salanter felt that "communities in Germany were already so far removed from Judaism that the time was ripe to bring them back."[10]

In the city of Koenigsburg he began to influence university students. He invited them to his home, where he lectured on Prophets, Talmud and musar. Rabbi Jacob Hirsch of Koenigsburg shared the lecture schedule with him. In Koenigsburg Rabbi Salanter published the pamphlet *Igeret ha-Musar* (*Letter of Musar*).

In 1860 Rabbi Salanter settled in the city of Mamel, near the Lithuanian border. There two eminent merchants, Benjamin Heineman and Elijahu Fishel, permitted him to use their homes for his work, and supported him in all his endeavors. Several university students in whom he took an interest became later leaders of German Jewry. Among these were Dr. Naphtali Eherman, Dr. Vilgimuth and others.

In Mamel, Rabbi Salanter began to publish a monthly periodical, "Hatvuna" ("Understanding"), stressing morality and ethical principles. Contributing to this publication were prominent rabbis from many countries, among them Rabbi Alexander Moshe Lapidus, Rabbi Eliezer Moshe Hurvitz, Rabbi Haim Berlin, the brothers Rabbi Yehiel and Rabbi Joshua Heller, Rabbi Joseph Dov Soloveichik, Rabbi Josef Saul Natanson, Rabbi Mordecai Gimbel, Rabbi Meir Aurebach and Rabbi Samuel Salant (from Jerusalem), Rabbi Zvi Kalischer, Rabbi Shlomo Kluger, and Rabbi Samuel Avigdor Tosfah, among others. The periodical ran from 1860 to 1861, and then had to stop because of technical reasons.

Rabbi Salanter did not limit his work in Germany to projects

---

[9]Dov Katz, *op. cit.*, I, p. 179.
[10]See Jacob Mark, *Gdolim Fun Unser Tzeit* (New York, 1927), p. 87.

in Koenigsburg and Mamel. He became a German citizen in order to be permitted to carry on his work. He mastered the German language and dressed like a German Jew, the more easily to exert his influence in spreading morality. He spent many months in Berlin, Frankfurt, Tilsit, Halberstadt, and other cities, and in every city he found supporters who helped him to recount the importance of musar, reverence and Torah knowledge. He was in close contact with the outstanding rabbis of Germany, in particular with Rabbi Ezriel Hildesheimer of Berlin, Rabbi Raphael Hirsch of Frankfurt, and Rabbi Meir Lehman of Maynce. There is no doubt that he made a vital contribution to bringing Torah Judaism back to Germany.

Rabbi Salanter, with the help of his students, established "Beth Midrashoth" (houses of learning) in many cities of Lithuania and Germany, for workers who came to pray and to study there. He also encouraged the education of girls in knowledge of the laws of Judaism.

The Kovna Academy of Higher Learning

In 1877 Rabbi Salanter established an academy of higher learning in Kovna, for the purpose of providing expert teachers in Torah and musar. The academy also accepted married students who wanted to pursue their studies further.

The academy was made possible by the ten-thousand-ruble contribution of Obediah Lachman and the arduous work of Rabbi Eliezer Jacob Chvas. It won the support of Rabbi Isaac Elhanan and Alexander Lapidus, who set up an organization to raise funds for it. Messengers were dispatched to surrounding cities to collect funds. Rabbi Baruch Zev, Rabbi Eliezer Jacob, and others were instrumental in obtaining the necessary funds.[11]

At the head of the Kovna academy were Rabbis Abraham Shenker, Nathan Zvi Finkel, and Zvi Rabinovitz. In 1880 Rabbi Rabinovitz took the position of rabbi in Midway Latvia. Rabbi Elhanan called a meeting to select new heads for the academy. The newly-apointed administrators were Rabbis Isaac Blazer, dean, and Rabbis Elijahu Markel and Baruch Broida, financial administrators. Under Rabbi Blazer's leadership the number of married students

---

[11]E. E. Friedman, op. cit., p. 133.

reached one hundred twenty. Among them were several well-known scholars: Rabbis Abraham Burstein, Zvi Mah-Yafith, Samuel Avigdor Fivolson, Joshua Klatzkin, Haim Rabinovitz, and others. When Rabbi Salanter visited the academy he participated in moral discussions with the students. He realized how difficult it was for a student to master every aspect of Jewish learning, therefore he advocated that students specialize in one field of Torah learnng, so that they might become expert in their fields.

The Periodical "Ha-Lebanon"

When the Enlightenment showed that it was trying to make changes in the religious institutions of the Jews, Rabbi Salanter moved swiftly to counterbalance these attempts. For instance, the periodicals "Ha-Meliz" ("Interpreter") and "Ha-Magid" ("Preacher") were abusive to rabbis and came out in favor of changes in religious observance. Therefore Rabbi Salanter felt it necessary to develop modern tools to invalidate the arguments of the Maskilim. The periodical "Ha-Lebanon" ("Lebanon"), published in Paris, answered this need by supporting the rabbis against the verbal attacks of the men of the Enlightenment.

When Moses Lilienblum came out against the Talmud in his article "Additions to the Path of the Talmud," Rabbi Salanter asked Rabbi Isaac Margoliot of Kovna to write a book. The book, *Strength of the Talmud,* was published with Rabbi Salanter's financial assistance.[12]

also chapter: *The Musar Movement and the Enlightenment* for more details.

It is paradoxical that the Maskilim did not mock or dishonor Rabbi Salanter, who was, so to speak, the "general in the battle against the Enlightenment."

> At a time when the enlighteners covered with dust all the rabbis and believers of the generation, as it is told, and they published certain books to insult them, they did not mention the name of Rabbi Israel and they did not dishonor him. . . . At the time the writer Abraham Mapu published his book *Ayit Tzabua (The Hypocrite)* , his enlightened friends scolded him for embarrassing Rabbi Israel through one of his characteristic scenes.[13]

---

[12]See Jacob Lipschitz, Sichron Jacob (Kannas-Slabada), II, pp. 94f. 123f. See
[13]Jacob Mark, *Gdolim Fun Unser Tzeit* (New York, 1927), p. 377.

The followers of the Enlightenment "praised [Rabbi Salanter] and said of him that he was a harbinger of place and time to give life to many souls and to spread true knowledge and sound morality."[14] One of the great writers of the Enlightenment, Kalman Shulman, said: "If there were in our time another man of his stature, there would be a revolution among the Jews."[15]

The second generation of Maskilim also thought highly of Rabbi Salanter. One of these, Nahum Sokolow, wrote the following:

> Indeed, his existence is not like our existence today; his ways are far apart from our ways. And only lofty ideas this outstanding man carried in his noble heart, and his spiritual paths are influential even now. He possessed a deep communal feeling; a people's conscience was beating in his heart, which took him out from the house of his study and made him a public servant of great energy, of strong determination. . . . Great he was in his spirit, in his morality, and in his thoughts.[16]

Rabbi Nahum Zev Zissel's Contribution

Rabbi Nahum Zev Zissel followed in the footsteps of Rabbi Salanter in his involvement in communal problems. Rabbi Zissel was a merchant all his life; nevertheless, he devoted six hours a day to the study of Torah and morality. He made time in his heavy schedule to visit the sick in the hospital each Sunday. His business acumen was made available to businessmen with serious financial difficulties.

During the First World War, Rabbi Zissel saved the entire city of Kelm from destruction by advising the inhabitants not to panic and run as the enemy approached. In Koenigsburg, he taught a Talmud class, and his spiritual and moral influence was great, particularly among the aristocratic German Jews. In 1910, he and his brother-in-law, Rabbi Zvi Broida, headed the Talmudical Academy of Kelm without drawing a salary. Rabbi Zissel showed remarkable skill for teaching and instilling morality in his students.

14*Ha-Shaha* (Vilna, 1880), Vol. 10, pp. 230-241.
15Told by Rabbi Nathan Zvi Finkel in Dov Katz, *op. cit.*, I, p. 212.
16Nahum Sokolow, *Ha-Tzfira* (Warsaw, sixth day of Cheshvan, 1931).

Rabbi Jeruham Levovitz, dean of the Mir Rabbinical Seminary, praised Rabbi Zissel as follows: "Through his wisdom and power of speech he was able to draw the whole world to morality, but he was very humble and thought of himself as unfit for such a task."[17]

Rabbi Moses Isaac's Contribution

Rabbi Moses Isaac was a gifted preacher of the Musar Movement. For almost fifty years he traveled from city to city, preaching musar among the Jews. He decried cheating in business and deceit in weights and measures. He spoke out vigorously against dishonesty in trade with Christians, calling it a crime and a defamation of the Jewish reputation. According to Rabbi Isaac, moral laxity in the business world was "not only a sin between man and man but also a severe breach in the foundations of the faith."[18]

---

[17]Told by J. Weinberg, who heard it from Rabbi J. Levovitz in Dov Katz, *op. cit.*, II, 104.
[18]*Ibid.*, p. 399.

CHAPTER 9

THE MUSAR MOVEMENT AND THE BOLSHEVIKS

Rabbi Joseph Yozel Hurwitz

From 1917 to 1920 Rabbi Joseph Yozel Hurwitz, of the Musar Movement, headed many rabbinical seminaries in the Soviet Union. His experiences under Communism and those of his students expose the tragic plight of religious Jews and theological institutions under the Soviets.

On one occasion Rabbi Hurwitz received a telegram from the seminary at Saratov stating that the Bolsheviks had ordered the seminary closed. His answer was to continue the study of Talmud and musar there—even under pain of death. Rabbi Y. L. Nekritz, presently a Rosh Yeshiva (head of a Yeshiva) at the Navaradock Yeshiva in Brooklyn, was there at the time. He said that when a group of soldiers entered the study hall, they confronted rabbis and students who were willing to die for the sake of keeping the doors of Torah learning open. Rabbi Nekritz was imprisoned by the Bolsheviks and was exiled to Siberia until 1945.

The Soviet Government prohibited the study of religion for persons under eighteen; converted synagogues to political and social clubs; persecuted rabbis and theology students; and devised other schemes to uproot religion. Despite this, the students of Rabbi Hurwitz at the Rabbinical Seminary of Navaradock continued their studies. They did more than that. They established new theological institutions in the Ukraine and White Russia of the Soviet Union. Later, however, realizing the grave danger confronting them in the heart of the Soviet Union, Rabbi Hurwitz and his students transferred their seminaries nearer the borders of Poland.[1]

At the same time the yeshivoth of Kharkov, Rostov, Nizhni-Novogorod and other cities in the heart of the Soviet Union moved to the surroundings of the Ukraine and White Russia, and settled in the cities of Mohilev, Bobroisk, Retzitzah, Zhitomir, Berdichev,

---

[1] Record of interview with Rabbi Y. L. Nekritz, October 13, 1967. See also Dov Katz, *Tenuath ha-Musar* (Tel Aviv, 1936), IV, pp. 223, 224.

Knotop, Mozir, Rogtzov, and others. The Communists interrupted the study of Talmud and musar in these locations also. There were public trials, and persecutions of the followers of the Torah. On several occasions students of Rabbi Hurwitz, either willingly or forcibly, went on trial as guilty of studying the teachings of the Torah or as defendants in other religious matters. The verdict in these cases, determined before the students took the stand, was "death for keeping and studying Judaism."[2]

In 1919 Rabbi Hurwitz made Kiev the center of his chain of yeshivoth. At this time, a time of civil war in the Soviet Union, the Ukraine became the main target for pogroms and antisemitism. The army bands of the anti-Soviet general Anton Denikin and Simon Petliura were guilty of pillaging and brutal atrocities against the Jews. It is a matter of record that from 1918 to 1921, as a result of the pogroms in the Ukraine, thirty thousand Jews were slain and 150,000 died later from wounds and contagious and other illnesses contracted during these disturbances. Twenty-eight percent of all Ukrainian Jewish houses were burned, and ten percent were abandoned by their owners.[3] The Bolsheviks, led by Lenin, were against anti-Semitism, therefore the Red Army appeared to be the more humane in its treatment of the Jews.[4] Many students of Rabbi Hurwitz were arrested by the White Russians (opponents of the Reds in the civil war). Others escaped by hiding in cellars and cemeteries, there to continue the study of Torah.[5]

Conditions in the Ukraine grew worse and worse for Rabbi Hurwitz and his students. Rabbi Hurwitz tried to instill courage in his students and in other Jews to face the attacks by the Whites with faith in God and in justice.

In addition to the violence of Denikin and Petliura, the Jews suffered heavy casualties from the plague that spread throughout Kiev, killing fifteen thousand people in the first three months of 1920. The plague was particularly tragic for refugees staying in the city's synagogues. These were converted to hospitals, and Rabbi

---

[2]Ibid.

[3]Salo W. Baron, *The Russian Jew under Tsars and Soivets* (New York, 1964), p. 221.

[4]Lenin, *Sochineniia*, 2nd ed. XXIV (1932), p. 203. Salo Baron, *op. cit.*, pp. 214-217.

[5]Dov Katz, *op. cit.*, IV, p. 224. Record of interview with Rabbi Y. L. Nekritz, October 13, 1967.

Hurwitz and his students ministered to the sick. An old woman, who had been bringing food to the sick, volunteered to assist them and wash the floors of their quarters, but was not permitted to do so, because Rabbi Hurwitz was afraid she also would become stricken with the disease. Instead, he and his disciples nursed the sick with dedication, until the plague took his own life in December of 1920.

Despite the danger of violence from antisemitic bands of White Russians stationed in Kiev, large numbers of Jews (among them many yeshiva students) came to pay their last respects to this great spiritual and moral leader of the Musar Movement. His outstanding disciple, Rabbi David Budnick, himself sick with a high temperature, rose from his bed to eulogize his beloved teacher.[6] He told his listeners that the motto of Rabbi Hurwitz had been that his students strive for justice all their lives. "[Rabbi Hurwitz] is not dead," concluded Rabbi Budnick, "but lives on in our midst." All of his students pledged the following:

> To keep his inheritance and to follow his noble path for-
> ever. To work with all their strength and enthusiasm and
> to stand like a rugged rock in the oasis of the sea to main-
> tain the existing seminaries and to establish new institu-
> tions of learning. . . . To carry the banner of Torah and
> God-fearing with pride and determination all the days.[7]

Rabbi Jaffan and the Bolsheviks

After the death of Rabbi Hurwitz, his son-in-law, Rabbi Abraham Jaffan, succeeded him as head of all of his established seminaries. Learning and musar were continued in the pattern set by the saintly teacher.[8]

The Communists once again began to harass the yeshivoth and the students of Rabbi Jaffan. Arrests of students became common. In the prisons, the determination to continue the study of Talmud and musar and the practice of religious rituals never ceased. In the

---

[6]Rabbi Y. L. Nekritz, *Yeshivath Navaradock-Beth Joseph* (New York, 1956), p. 260; record of interview with Rabbi Nekritz, October 13, 1967. See also Dov Katz, *op. cit.*, pp. 225, 226.

[7]See *Or ha-Musar* (St. Petersburg, 1926), No. 11. See also Dov Katz, *op. cit.*, p. 226f.

[8]Rabbi Y. L. Nekritz, *op. cit.*, p. 260f.

prison of Minsk, students were given pages of Talmud and books of morality placed in the wrappings of herring so that the Bolshevik guards would not seize them.[9]

At the end of 1921 Rabbi Jaffan and ten of his best students, who were members of the yeshiva administration, were arrested, accused of spreading Torah and influencing sons of Jewish Communists. (Many sons of Jewish Communists were attracted to yeshivoth and studied Torah enthusiastically.)

In jail, Rabbi Jaffan and his students were tormented by constant interrogation. Rabbi Jaffan was pressed to reveal the "secret" of the students' influence upon the youth and to reveal the names of yeshiva leaders in the surroundings of Homel. The Bolsheviks wanted him to sign a document of his guilt and to submit his resignation as head of the network of yeshivoth. Rabbi Jaffan was able to argue himself out of doing so, but even so his best students were not freed from prison. They were forced, like political criminals, to do hard labor. Rabbi Jaffan and his students felt obligated to carry on the teachings of the Torah in spite of grave danger. They felt that the Communists' policy of religious persecution could lead only to assimilation and conversion.[10]

Rabbi Kagan's Advice

After two years of persecution, imprisonment, and danger, Rabbi Jaffan and his disciples turned to Rabbi Israel Meir Kagan for advice.[11] Rabbi Kagan recommended that they emigrate to Poland, and they did so in 1922.

It was not easy to leave Russia. Borders had to be crossed illegally. Rabbi Jaffan and his followers divided into small groups and hid in the mountains, in the forests, and in the fields. Some groups were caught and imprisoned, and after leaving prison tried again to cross the borders. The main arteries that were used for illegal trespass were Novogorod, Wilinsk, and Baranowitz.[12] Those who crossed safely into Poland were greeted by Jews with food and clothing.

---

[9] See Dov Katz, *op. cit.*, p. 227.
[10] See Rabbi Y. L. Nekritz, *op. cit.*, p. 264.
[11] See the introduction of Rabbi Jaffan to "Matragat ha-Adam" (New York, 1947).
[12] See Y. L. Nekritz, *op. cit.*, p. 265f.

Once they were established in Poland, Rabbi Jaffan and his followers began to set up seminaries. Rabbi Jaffan himself headed the main seminary at Bialystok. Rabbi David Blicher established a seminary in Mezritz. Rabbi Abraham Zalmans and Rabbi David Budnick set up institutions in Warsaw and Dvinsk Latvia. Rabbi Samuel Weintrieb was in charge of a seminary in the city of Simiatitz. Soon all of these institutions were sending students out to found new seminaries. Prior to the Second World War Rabbi Jaffan headed sixty institutions with an enrollment of thousands of students. The chain of seminaries was called "Beth Joseph" ("House of Joseph") in honor of Rabbi Joseph Yozel Hurwitz.[13]

The Kagan-Grodzenski Letters

In the year 1930, Rabbi Israel Meir Kagan and Rabbi Hayyim Ozer Grodzenski of Vilna wrote the following letter, entitled "Voice Calls":

> According to the report that came, the heart faints and the hands tremble. Approximately three million Jews are in captivity under distress and oppression. Several tens of thousands of Jews, with their families, were banished from their homes in the middle of the winter; they are scattered in the street and are starving, and besides the physical destruction that left the majority of the Jews there without economic security, they, our brothers, experience religious persecution.[14]

In a second letter in 1930, the two relate the following:

> Holy scrolls, books of the Talmud, phylacteries, and the scrolls at the door posts are being burned in the streets; houses of study are being converted to theaters and saloons; ritual baths are closed and the keeping of the family purity laws is being abandoned. The Communists compel the Jews to desecrate the Sabbath; and many of the Rabbis and Torah scholars are being sentenced to prison; and many of the rabbis and Torah scholars are exiled to Siberia.[15]

---

[13]*Ibid.*, pp. 226-269.

[14]Letter from Rabbi Kagan and Rabbi Grodzenski, Adar, 1930, in *Michtavei Hafets Hayyim*, II, pp. 56-57.

[15]Letter from Rabbi Kagan and Rabbi Grodzenski, Adar, 1930, in *Ibid.*, II, pp. 57-60.

In 1931, in a letter to rabbis and communal leaders, they wrote:

> Behold, the miserable condition of our unfortunate and
> oppressed brothers in the Soviet Government is known;
> their economic root has been destroyed completely; and
> many hundreds and thousands of Jews are lacking bread
> and are suffering from starvation; general aid is prohibited,
> but it is possible to send food packages to individuals . . .
> and already prominent rabbis have been informed to stress
> the necessity of sending packages which truthfully save
> lives.[16]

The two rabbis urged that packages be dispatched not only during the year but also on holidays, and that every Jew who knew
the address of a relative or friend should send the package himself to the Soviet Union. Jews who did not have such addresses
could send the money to the Relief Bureau in Vilna or to Rabbi
Kagan or Rabbi Grodzenski.

Rabbi Kagan and Rabbi Grodzenski were two of the most respected spiritual leaders in the world in their time. They used their
international influence to help, as much as was possible, the unfortunate Jews behind the Iron Curtain.

Their letters, together with the experiences of Rabbi Hurwitz
and Rabbi Jaffan, portray the sadness of Russian Jewry.

---

[16]Letter from Rabbi Kagan and Rabbi Grodzenski, Elul, 1931, in *Ibid.*, II, pp.
197-198.

CHAPTER 10

THE MAIN EDUCATIONAL INSTITUTIONS OF THE MUSAR MOVEMENT AND THEIR DISTINCT MODES OF THOUGHT

Introduction

When Rabbi Israel Salanter died in 1883, the future of the Musar Movement seemed doubtful. The seminary for married students in Kovna and similar establishments in other localities had emerged under the auspices of the local communities. The fate of musar would appear doomed under such a "public" setup, with the conflicts and controversy that the term implies, but in reality it was strengthened by communal tensions, because under these circumstances the educational musar institutions withdrew into privacy—and in so doing insured their development.

Rabbi Salanter's six outstanding disciples were Rabbi Simhah Zissel Ziv Braude (1829-1898), who was known as "Der Alter" of Kelm; Rabbi Naphtali Amsterdam (1832-1916); Rabbi Isaac Blazer (1837-1907); Rabbi Jacob Joseph (1848-1902); Rabbi Joseph Yozel Hurwitz (1848-1919), "Der Alter" of Navaradock; and Rabbi Nathan Zvi Hirsch Finkel (1849-1928), "Der Alter" of Slobodca.[1]

In this chapter, the three personalities who founded distinct musar schools and earned the title "Der Alter" (Elder) will be discussed.

The Kelm School and its Founder, Rabbi Simhah Zissel

Rabbi Simhah Zissel was born in Kelm, Lithuania, to a scholarly family.[2] He received a thorough traditional Orthodox Jewish education in his youth. He also studied in Kovna under Rabbi Salanter.[3]

---

[1]Dov Katz, *Tenuath ha-Musar* (Tel Aviv, Zioni, 1954-1963), Vols. II, III, IV. This work provides valuable information on the life and works of Rabbi Salanter's closest followers, some of which is based on primary sources and the accounts of eyewitnesses.

[2]Eliezer E. Friedman, *Sefer ha-Zichronoth (1858-1926)* (Tel Aviv, Achdut, 1926), p. 10f. Eliezer E. Friedman was born in Kelm and was an eyewitness to the rise of the Musar Movement in general and to the Kelm school in particular. His memoirs are objective and reliable, providing an indispensable primary source for the Musar Movement as well as for the life and works of Rabbi Simhah Zissel.

[3]*Ibid.*, p. 77.

Rabbi Simhah Zissel told of his first encounter with Rabbi Salanter:

> When he heard that a house of musar was established in Kovna, he did not understand its nature or its need. He went to Kovna with a critical attitude toward the house of musar. After he heard Rabbi Salanter's talk, he decided to remain there and for a full year he was engrossed only in the study of musar.[4]

Rabbi Salanter guided him to concentrate particularly on character-building. "And I am still," Rabbi Simhah Zissel used to say, "on this portion and [have worked] arduously on character-building from the time of my encounter with Rabbi Salanter until now."[5]

Rabbi Simhah Zissel, with his probing mind and mystical nature, became one of Rabbi Salanter's closest confidants. Rabbi Salanter had great confidence in him and hoped that he would disseminate his own views on Judaism and musar among Orthodox laity. Rabbi Salanter's dreams soon materialized.[6]

After Rabbi Salanter left Russia for Germany in 1857, Rabbi Simhah Zissel became the pillar of the Musar Movement, and it is really with him that the history of the musar study house begins. He set these up in Kovna and Vilna in accordance with Rabbi Salanter's ideas. He also established places where an ordinary Jew could go for an hour of study and contemplation, or to listen to a musar sermon.

During Rabbi Simhah Zissel's stay in Kovna, three leading rabbis, Leib Schapiro, Heschel of Yanova, and Isiah of Salant, began a protest against the house of musar in Kovna. They feared that the new movement would disrupt Jewish religious life.[7] Rabbi Heschel of Yanova, who was well known for his preaching, was sent by Rabbi Schapiro to the musar house where Rabbi Salanter

---

[4]Told by Rabbi Elijahu Eliezer Dessler in the name of his father, Rabbi Reuven Dov Dessler in Dov Katz, *Tenuath ha-Musar*, *op. cit.*, II, 30.

[5]Told by Rabbi Moses Resnick and others in Dov Katz, *Tenuath ha-Musar*, *Ibid.*

[6]Eliezer E. Friedman, "Toldoth Baalei ha-Musar" in *Ha-Meliz*, No. III, 1897. This was an article on the evolution of the Musar Movement with emphasis on the personalities of Simhah Zissel and Israel Salanter as well as the musar houses in Kelm, Kovna and Slobodca. The article is a valuable primary source.

[7]Eliezer E. Friedman, *Sefer ha-Zichronoth*, *op. cit.*, p. 80. See also Friedman, "Toldoth Baalei ha-Musar" in *Ha-Meliz*, No. 108, 1897.

lectured, to refute his musar talks.[8] Rabbi Simhah Zissel defended the Musar Movement against the critics with the following argument:

> Let no one think that the protesters are right because they are in the majority. It is not so; for, if a person has not studied musar, his understanding is not considered, just as the opinion of a person who has not studied medicine is not important in the sick case.[9]

He also said that through learning and practicing morality, one could achieve a true fear of the Almighty.

Rabbi Simhah Zissel's birthplace, Kelm, was renowned for Jewish learning and Mithnagdism (non-Hasidism), and had an unusually large number of Talmudic scholars. When Rabbi Simhah Zissel returned to Kelm after being away for many years, its numbers had increased. Families had come from frontier towns, where their right of residence had been denied by the government. (It will be remembered that under Tsar Nicholas I, Jews were forbidden to dwell in villages as well as in frontier towns.)

The newcomers were looked upon with disdain by the haughty and scholarly Jews of Kelm, whose families had lived there for generations. They felt forlorn, and appreciated any show of friendliness. Rabbi Simhah Zissel took up the cause of uniting these immigrants, and he drew his first followers from them.[10] He became their spiritual leader. He told his followers in sermons that in addition to studying Torah they must devote time to the study of musar, so that character-building, fear of God, and noble thoughts would be part of their personality.[11] In this way the new families were imbued with a sense of dignity and self-respect. Twelve men from among them soon emerged as his closest confidants, with Sholem Ziv, Raphael Greenberg, Avraham Zelter, and Avraham Yavneh as the most outstanding.[12] His devoted followers campaigned for new

---

[8]Rabbi Simhah Zissel wrote this in a letter to one of his friends. See Dov Katz, *Tenuath ha-Musar, op. cit.,* p. 77f.

[9]Eliezer E. Friedman, *Sefer ha-Zichronoth, op. cit.,* p. 78. See also Friedman, "Toldoth Baalei ha-Musar" in *Ha-Meliz,* No. 111, 1897.

[10]*Ibid.*

[11]*Ibid.,* p. 78.

[12]*Ibid.*

disciples and spread the news of the greatness and holiness of Rabbi Simhah Zissel.[13]

The Beth Hatalmud of Kelm

Rabbi Simhah Zissel and his followers founded a yeshiva, the Beth Hatalmud of Kelm, in 1874. The first floor was for prayer and study and also served as sleeping quarters for those who needed them. Rabbi Simhah Zissel had his study on the second floor, which was also used as the central office of the Kelm followers of the Musar Movement. The room on the top floor was used by musar leaders for private meetings. It was considered a great honor to gain entrance there, and one needed an invitation to come.[14] Many students were attracted to the Beth Hatalmud, including sons of the rich from different localities. Students were placed in classes where Hebrew, Talmud, and Russian were taught.[15] Many, however, left to study in the yeshiva of Rabbi Eliezer Gordon,[16] who devoted more time to Talmud study than to musar.[17] In Rabbi Simhah Zis- There was some protest from the townspeople because the students were so engrossed in musar and its practice, had to devote more time than seemed necessary to prayers, and spent too much time in meditation and self-analysis and listening to Rabbi Simhah Zissel's lengthy sermons and talks.

He brought innovations into the yeshiva that must indeed have perturbed the Orthodox Jews of Kelm. On the Sabbath, for instance, the students prayed Shaharith (the morning service) and read the Torah and then, instead of praying Musaph (the additional service after the Torah reading), went home for lunch. *Then* they returned for Musaph[19]—and the study of musar. On the Day

---

13*Ibid.*

14*Ibid.*, p. 81.

15*Ibid.*

16Rabbi Eliezer Gordon (1841-1910) was a contemporary of Rabbi Simhah Zissel and became spiritual leader of Kelm in 1874. In 1885, he became spiritual leader of Telshe, and also headed the famous Telshe Yeshiva. An excellent source of his life and works is "Ha-Gaon Rabbi Eliezer Gordon" in Eliezer E. Friedman, *Sefer ha-Zichronoth.*

17*Ibid.*, pp. 99-101. See also Eliezer E. Friedman, "Toldoth Baalei ha-Musar" in *Ha-Meliz*, No. 111, 1897.

sel's yeshiva, musar was stressed as part of the curriculum.[18]

18*Ibid.*, p. 81, and Friedman, *Ibid.*

19There were additional offerings in the Sabbath and Festival services, over and above the regular daily morning prayers.

Levitan, Isaac Meltzen and others lectured there, and the "Court of Strauss" became the center of musar in Jerusalem.

of Atonement, to give another example, the musar students broke the fast after the Neilah service[20] instead of after Maariv (the evening prayer) as is usually the custom. These innovations may have had merit, but unfortunately they were considered "reforms." Townspeople withdrew their support from the Beth Hatalmud. Many students preferred to devote more time to the study of Talmud than to musar doctrines, and so they either transferred to Rabbi Eliezer Gordon's yeshiva or left Kelm altogether.

In 1876, the Russian authorities were informed that the Beth Hatalmud of Kelm was a center for rebellious activities against the Tsarist Government. The police conducted an investigation which lasted for many years, and Rabbi Salanter urged Rabbi Simhah Zissel to open a school in another town.[21] When the townspeople displayed their displeasure by withdrawing their support of the Beth Hatalmud, Rabbi Simhah Zissel moved the school to Grobin.[22]

The Yeshiva in Grobin

In the town of Grobin, Courland, Rabbi Simhah Zissel established a yeshiva which taught Hebrew as well as the secular subjects required by the government. This institution was oriented to educate the children of the rich, who were pleased with the high standards of learning and were willing to contribute to the upkeep of the school. One of the prominent supporters of the yeshiva was Eliezer Dessler, whose nephews studied there. He contributed eleven thousand rubles for the construction of a new yeshiva in Grobin.

The administrators were Rabbi Nathan Zvi Finkel and Rabbi Elijahu Zvi Lizrowitz. Prominent members of the faculty were Rabbi Zvi Offenheim, who was later appointed Rabbi of Kelm on the recommendation of Rabbi Simhah Zissel; Rabbi Eliezer Levy, who served for a long time as Rabbi of Tzitiwan, Lithuania, and who in his old age settled in Jerusalem; Rabbi Smarjahu Bloch, who

---

20Neilah is the conclusion service on the Day of Atonement. The word literally means "the closing of the gates."

21Told by Rabbi Chaim Shraga Levin, a contemporary of Rabbi Simhah Zissel, in Dov Katz, *op. cit.*, II, 65.

22Eliezer E. Friedman, "Toldoth Baalei ha-Musar" in *Ha-Meliz*, No. III, 1897.

was later named Rabbi of London; Rabbi Ben Zion Karnitz, and others.

The burden of running the yeshiva at Grobin finally caused Rabbi Simhah Zissel to become ill, and in 1886 he was forced to close the school.[23]

Once more the Beth Hatalmud at Kelm became a center for musar learning. The emphasis was on quality; only outstanding students were admitted. Rabbi Simhah Zissel writes: "I hesitate to will quantity, but I will to increase quality. . . . I desire to devote myself to those who do not think of themselves, money, and honor. If I shall find such students, I would dedicate myself physically and spiritually in their behalf."[24]

Local as well as outside support was given to the Beth Hatalmud of Kelm, whose budget was not as high as that of the yeshiva at Grobin. One of the most eminent benefactors was Samuel Strauss, who donated six thousand rubles.[25]

During this time the Beth Hatalmud of Kelm reached the highest standards possible in the education of its students, who became known for their excellence in the study of Talmud and musar, and for achieving unusual ethical traits. The students of Rabbi Simhah Zissel assumed positions of leadership in spreading Torah and musar among the Jews in many cities in Russia as well as in the Holy Land.[26]

"Guardian of Musar"

Rabbi Simhah Zissel by no means confined his interests to the Beth Hatalmud. On the contrary, he devoted time and energy to the strengthening of God-fearing and musar outside the yeshiva environment. He saw himself as the "guardian of musar." He wrote: "Behold, the majority of the world feels cool toward musar. In spite of this, I will be a guardian of musar in order to extend its frontiers of influence, because I know that knowledge without morality is like soup without salt."[27]

---

[23]See letter of Rabbi Simhah Zissel to Rabbi Salanter, 1881, in Dov Katz, *Ibid.*, 67f.

[24]Letter from Rabbi Simhah Zissel in Dov Katz, *op. cit.*, II, 70f.

[25]*Ibid.*, p. 71.

[26]For the names of those in this highly select group, see Dov Katz, *Ibid.*, p. 72f.

[27]Letter from Rabbi Simhah Zissel in "Or ha-Musar" (Petrikov, 1928), vol. 13. See also Dov Katz, *op. cit.*, II, p. 73f.

He was constantly in touch with his former students, and was able to exert his influence upon them. He was active in strengthening musar in the yeshivoth of Slobodca, Telz, Radun, Mir, and elsewhere, where his former students were now spiritual leaders. He sent them musar material, feeling that though the Torah was the life of the Jewish people, they must strive to achieve morality by uprooting bad traits.[28]

In 1882, he was successful in establishing an organization for spreading musar in Palestine. Several of his students, Rabbi Boruch Marcus, Rabbi Samuel Schenker, and others, set up a musar school in Jerusalem which attracted, among others, the following outstanding students: Rabbis Abraham Hisin, Elijahu Lando, David Kovner, Zerech Epstein, Haim Mann, Jehiel Michal Tiktzinski, Jehiel Michal Mushkin, Yudel Mirer, Ididya Horodner, Yonah Rom, and Jacob Moshe Harlap.[29]

In 1897 his followers established the Yeshiva Or Hadas (New Light) for unmarried students in Jerusalem. Musar held a prominent place on the curriculum, and well-known rabbis gathered there to study Torah in an atmosphere of holiness and purity. Baron Edmond de Rothschild and Samuel Strauss provided the funds necessary for the establishment of the yeshiva. In the course of the proceedings Rabbi Simhah Zissel persuaded Strauss to become a follower of the Musar Movement. He prevailed upon Strauss to construct a large house for the yeshiva and for housing the followers of the Musar Movement. The house has been known till this day as the "Court of Strauss." Such famous leaders of the Musar Movement as Rabbis Isaac Blazer, Naphtali Amsterdam, Leib Broida, Zvi

Rabbi Simhah Zissel was delighted with his success in the Holy Land, and he saw in it the "beginning of redemption." In his letters to his followers he urged them to take upon themselves the task of disseminating Torah and musar.[30]

Contemporary School of Thought

The Kelm school of thought is better understood in light of contemporary thought. Rabbi Simhah Zissel's times were marked on the one hand by the influence of the Haskalah, which, as we

---

[28]Told by Moshe Sharevsky, a student of Simhah Zissel, in Dov Katz, *Ibid.,* II, p. 77.
[29]*Ibid.,* p. 83.
[30]*Ibid.,* p. 84.

have seen, called for secular education; and on the other hand the dry, pilpulistic method of Talmud study.[31] In other words, there was no curriculum available which took into consideration the "whole student"—his religious, ethical, educational and social development, matters over which the Maskilim and the religious Jews could not even start constructive talk.[32]

In Kelm, the well-educated, religious Jews looked down upon the poorer, newly-arrived Jews.[33] Rabbi Simhah Zissel, like the Baal Shem Tov himself (the founder of Hasidism), made it his business to attract these poor Jews to the Musar Movement. The poor Jews of Kelm were ill prepared to understand the pilpulistic sermons and Talmudic discourses so dear to the hearts of the scholars in the town.[34] Thus, Rabbi Simhah Zissel brought meaningful education and musar to the poor as well as to the rich. He was not against the teaching of secular subjects provided the priority was on Torah and musar. He was not against pilpul in the study of Talmud —provided students were also grounded in musar.

The Kelm School of Thought

The Musar Movement, then, became known for its three major schools of thought: the Kelm school; the Slobodca school under Rabbi Nathan Zvi Finkel; and the Navaradock school of Rabbi Joseph Yozel Hurwitz. Each of these three worked according to his own views. Each was responsible for educating thousands of Jews to be God-fearing and moral.

The Kelm school of thought was the first one to be coordinated into a system which called for the perfection of man. It was not a body of philosophical ideas; rather, it encompassed the whole development of man from his elementary education until his full self-realization, teaching a way of life.[35]

The main emphasis of the Kelm school of thought was on applied education, stressing concrete practices and self-betterment, with the role of the individual of prime importance. Rabbi Simhah Zissel felt that improvement in man could come through education;

---

[31]See Chapter: *The Musar Movement and the Enlightenment*. Pilpulistic method involves casuistic subtlety in the study of Talmud.

[32]*Ibid.*

[33]Eliezer E. Friedman, *Sefer ha-Zichronoth, op. cit.*, p. 78.

[34]*Ibid.*

[35]*Ibid.*, p. 121.

hence a person must dedicate himself to education.[36] Man was created to pursue learning, which has no end. The purpose of education should be to achieve during one's lifetime the fearing of God.[37] An individual must acquire the habit of study in his youth so that he will be used to it in his middle years and old age. Thus the Kelm school of reasoning.

It further taught that thinking was one of the most significant ways to attain education, since this distinguishes man from other living creatures. Thinking was what enabled man to act according to reason, wisdom and understanding. Study should be accompanied by an awakening: an awakening of happiness for a happy occasion, and a sad awakening for a plaintive one. All learning should take the form of an examination: "How have I thought and what now have I learned?"[38] A student must be able to strip the wisdom from a given text to produce creative wisdom.[39]

Since man's powers of reflection and observation are his weapons in his struggles against animalistic tendencies, Rabbi Simhah Zissel held that "the person who neglects his reflective faculties commits spiritual suicide."[40] He held that self-analysis must be accompanied by study of the world of things and people:[41] "The entire world is a Beth ha-Musar and each person is a musar book."[42]

According to Rabbi Simhah Zissel, most people retain their childhood concepts of good and evil, of religion and their environment. Since attitudes and views formed in childhood change little in later life in spite of the acquisition of new moral knowledge, there exists a gap between knowing and doing. It was thought by Rabbi Simhah Zissel and his followers that systematic thinking plus Rabbi Salanter's teachings had the power to break childhood habit formations and thought patterns.[43]

In summarizing the Kelm school of thought, one may say that it called for a synthesis of three basic objectives: *Torah*—to be studied with total concentration and dedication; *musar*—for the de-

---

[36]Rabbi Simhah Zissel, *Hokhma Umusar* (New York, Aber Press, Inc., 1957), I, p. 211f.
[37]See *Ibid.*, I, 398.
[38]*Ibid.*, I, 398f. See also Dov Katz, *op. cit.*, II, 126.
[39]See *Ibid.*, p. 401.
[40]See *Hokhma Umusar*, p. 137.
[41]*Ibid.*, p. 386.
[42]*Ibid.*, pp. 380-388.
[43]*Ibid.*, pp. 380-383.

velopment of an ethical "self"; and *general studies*—to acquaint the student with, and help him to adjust to, his physical, social, and economic conditions, as well as to prepare him to earn a livelihood.

The Kelm Curriculum

Rabbi Simhah Zissel's curriculum in the Beth Hatalmud of Kelm and in Grobin consisted of some secular and religious subjects. Only those familiar with the educational and social climate in nineteenth-century Russia can fully appreciate the importance of this innovation in the curriculum of the Jewish school. It was revolutionary not only in Lithuania but in all of Russia.

To be sure, Rabbi Simhah Zissel devoted more time to religious subjects than to general studies, but the significant fact here is that he did not consider the latter a "necessary evil." On the contrary. He believed that a knowledge of science and the general environment was necessary—not only for better living but for better comprehension of religious teachings as well.[44]

The curriculum called for strict adherence to order, discipline, cleanliness, and decorum, much more than was customary in those days. Rules were strictly enforced, without distinction between poor and rich students.[45]

Deserving students had their names recorded in a "White Book." Students who committed offenses had theirs inscribed in a "Black Book." The offenders made every effort to atone, so that their names might be erased. The books had considerable influence on all the students.[46]

Vaad (student body) proceedings had been initiated by Rabbi Salanter and were now refined by Rabbi Simhah Zissel. Group-analysis sessions were conducted in a spirit of equality and friendship. Each member of the group was concerned with the development of proper conduct patterns. The group was run democratically, with an older student serving as chairman. It issued regulations regarding decorum, proper speech, and dress.

In the Beth Hatalmud students were admitted and ranked on the basis of their moral attainments, while in other yeshivoth they were evaluated according to their scholastic achievements. The cur-

---

[44]Rabbi Simhah Zissel, *Hokhma Umusar, op. cit.,* I, p. 423f.
[45]Dov Katz, *op. cit.,* II, p. 184.
[46]*Ibid.,* p. 202.

riculum of Kelm tried to apply to practice the Kelm school of thought, in order that the student might be a good Jew and a well-adjusted human anywhere in the world.[47]

The Kelm School After Rabbi Simhah Zissel's Death

After Rabbi Simhah Zissel's death in 1898 no changes were made in the curriculum of the Beth Hatalmud. From 1898 to 1901 Rabbi Simhah Zissel's brother, Rabbi Leib, headed the school. For two years after his death Rabbi Isaac Blazer came to the Beth Hatalmud during the month of Elul and for the High Holidays, maintaining the high moral and spiritual life of the school.[48]

From 1901 to 1913 Rabbi Zvi Braude, Rabbi Leib's son and the son-in-law of Rabbi Simhah Zissel, and an outstanding pupil at the Beth Hatalmud, headed the school. Rabbi Nahum Zev, the son of Rabbi Simhah Zissel, became its head from 1913-1916. An excellent Talmudic scholar and a man of high character, he maintained the reputation of excellence in Torah and musar study at the Beth Hatalmud.[49]

After the death of Rabbi Nahum Zev, the Beth Hatalmud was headed by Rabbi Reuven Dessler, Rabbi Daniel Moshovitz, and Rabbi Gerson Miadnik (the latter two sons-in-law of Rabbi Nahum Zev).

During the Second World War, the Beth Hatalmud was destroyed and its students killed by the Nazis. The Kelm school of musar, initiated by Rabbi Simhah Zissel and continued for seventy-five years, came to an end. It was unable to put down roots in America or in Palestine, in spite of the efforts of Rabbi Elijahu Eliezer Dessler, a son-in-law of Rabbi Nahum Zev and a Beth Hatalmud student, who went on to hold the position of masgiah musari (overseer in musar) at the Poniviz Yeshiva in Israel.[50]

The Literature of the Kelm School of Thought

Rabbi Simhah Zissel was a prolific writer of articles and letters which reveal his thoughts and attitudes toward the religious, edu-

---

[47]*Ibid.*, pp. 176-192.
[48]Told by Rabbi Elijahu Dushnizer, a student at the Beth Hatalmud at that time, in Dov Katz, *Ibid.*, p. 89.
[49]*Ibid.*
[50]*Ibid.*

cational and social conditions of his time. In 1957 the first volume of *Hokhma Umusar,* which contains hundreds of these articles and letters, was published.[51] This volume is indispensable as primary source material. The second volume was published in 1964.

One can also find many of Rabbi Simhah Zissel's writings in *Sefer Or ha-Musar,* Volumes I and II, published in 1965 and 1966 by the Navaradock Yeshivoth. Dov Katz's *Tenuath ha-Musar* contains excellent primary source material on the Kelm school. The author had access to the manuscripts of Rabbi Simhah Zissel as well as to those of his contemporaries, living and dead.

Eliezer E. Friedman's articles in *Sefer ha-Zichronoth* and in *Ha-Meliz* (1897) are of great importance in discussing the origin of the Kelm school.

A sample of Rabbi Simhah Zissel's numerous articles and letters have been translated by the author, to give an idea of the primary source and its value for our times.

If I am for Myself, What am I?

> To my dear son. . . . I received your dear letter and I regretfully read about your illness . . . God, with His abundant mercy, will send you a full recovery from Heaven . . . so that you would continue to do kindness to the many. . . .
>
> The following topic was discussed after the evening prayer: What is kindness to others? Although Rahab did kindness to two men, it was considered as if she did it to all the Jews, otherwise, how could the two spies promise her that all the Israelites would not kill her family? Surely, the two men represented the opinion of the majority among the Jews, therefore, it is as if she did kindness to all the Jews. Now, we understand how important it is to preoccupy ourselves with deeds of kindness to the many.
>
> We also discussed what it means to understand a matter fully. All the nations heard what Rahab heard: that God dried up the Red Sea . . . as it is explained there, and even the King of Jericho heard it, and therefore why did he chase after the spies? Even if he captured them, behold: there is no way to stop the help of God. Surely, Rahab un-

---

[51]Rabbi Simhah Zissel, *Hokhma Umusar, op. cit.,* I, pp. 1-8.

derstood it fully because she decided to convert to Judaism and deserved to marry Joshua, second to Moses, and to have prophets as descendants. . . .

What does a noble feeling do for a man? Her kindness to the representatives of the many merited her to marry the leader of the many and to have children as prophets. . . . Live a purposeful life, says the one who blesses you. . . .[52]

How Long Does One Halt between Two Opinions?

Understand please, brothers, is there greater riches than from following the advice of this article? . . .

It is told that there was once a poverty-stricken philosopher and the king gave him much gold and silver to save him from the hardships of penury. He rose in the morning and took along with him the money, and he came before the king. He told him that he did not desire his money. The king became astounded and told him: Why have you done this to me, why have you rejected my gift which I presented to you? The philosopher replied: My master, from the day that I was born until this day, I had peace of mind while awake and while asleep since I did not covet riches and always I was satisfied with my lot, and all my wisdom was used to understand the wisdom of nature and to investigate its mysteries. . . . Since yesterday when I took the money I began to turn to vanities, by thinking, what should I do with the money? Should I buy merchandise with it to carry on a business, or is it better for me to leave it with an honest man, or should I buy property with which to provide a livelihood for my family? Sleep became impossible and difficulties surround me . . . and I am trapped between two philosophies of life. Since I cannot live such a life, I am returning the money to you. . . . You know, my dear son, how difficult it is for me to write, thus I was not lazy today to copy the words of this philosopher . . . See, my son, we are like a shameful thief, embarrassed and humiliated. How far we are removed from this heathen philosopher, because of our avaricious ma-

---

[52]Rabbi Simhah Zissel, "If I am for Myself, What am I?" in *Hokhma Umusar, op. cit.,* I, p. 16.

terialistic appetites. . . . We in this world always follow
two paths. Who knows, God forbid, what could happen
if we follow two paths? Just so, the philosopher learned
that night the consequences of two opinions. . . . How
unfortunate is a man who follows two paths.

Also, Elijahu the prophet advised the Jews to stop following two separate opinions. . . . We must correct this
evil through righteousness.[53]

Standards of Behavior

We must set up standards of behavior . . .and if we take
upon us these regulations, the merit will be big, forgive-
ness will be bestowed upon all Jewish people. He who desires to keep all of them, how good is he! He who wishes
to keep some . . . must keep them.

1. To set a fixed time for Torah study, every day or a
   few days a week, without an interruption of the schedule.
2. To be very careful during a certain period of each
   day or several times a week in the prevention of gossip.
3. To devote on each Sabbath at least an hour to the complete sanctity of the Sabbath by abstaining from idle
   conversation. If such conversation is a must on the Sabbath, one should use the Hebrew language as the ve-
   hicle of communication.
4. At least once a week a person must meditate on the
   mitzvah "Love thy neighbor as thyself."
5. At least once a week a person must open his heart
   to the mitzvah of gemiluth hesed—doing kindness to
   others.
6. At least once a week a person must practice the golden
   rule that actions speak louder than words.
7. At least once a week a person must rise diligently from
   his bed, just like a soldier, in order to engross himself
   in a sacred duty.

---

[53]Rabbi Simhah Zissel, "How Long Does One Halt between Two Opinions?"
in *Hokhma Umusar, Ibid.*, I, p. 51.

8. To abstain from unnecessary talk in a synagogue . . . during eating, during musar study, and in groups devoted to other noble causes.

9. For at least a half hour each day a Jew must study Torah in the company of another Jew.[54]

[54]Rabbi Simhah Zissel, "Standards of Behavior" in *Or ha-Musar*, (Bnei Brak, 1965), I, 248f.

CHAPTER 11

THE NAVARADOCK SCHOOL AND ITS FOUNDER, RABBI JOSEPH HURWITZ

Rabbi Joseph Yozel Hurwitz was born in Kortowian, in the district of Kovna. His father, Rabbi Shlomo Zalman Ziv Hurwitz, was the spiritual leader of Kortowian and was known as a righteous man and a Talmudic scholar. In his youth, Joseph Hurwitz displayed determination and sharpness in his studies. At eighteen he married a woman from Sveksne, a town adjacent to the Prussian border. In the interval betwen the betrothal and the marriage, his father-in-law passed away, leaving behind a widow and eight small children. Joseph Hurwitz undertook the responsibility of supporting the whole family. He entered the business world, from time to time making business trips to the port city of Mamel.

At that time Rabbi Israel Salanter made his home in Mamel, and taught Torah and musar. Rabbi Salanter once met Joseph Hurwitz when the latter was on his way to make a business deal. He stopped him and asked him, "Young man, why are you in such a hurry and what is your destination?" They conversed, and became friends. From then on, Joseph Hurwitz made frequent trips to Mamel to listen to Rabbi Salanter's musar talks.

Rabbi Hurwitz told his students: "Thirteen sermons I heard from Rabbi Israel in Mamel. After the thirteenth sermon, my outlook on life changed and I decided to abandon the business world in order to join a selective group, one preoccupied with the study of Torah and musar."[1]

He informed his family of this decision, handing them eight hundred rubles, a very large sum of money at that time. His father, his wife, and the rest of the family objected to this "leave of absence," but no one was able to change his mind, and he left for Mamel.[2] There, he was in contact with Rabbi Nathan Zvi Finkel, the founder of the Slobodca Yeshiva, Rabbi Eliezer Sulbitz, the

---

[1]Yehuda Leib Nekritz, *Yeshivath Navaradock* (New York, 1956), pp. 247-248.
[2]*Ibid.*

131

founder of the Lomza Yeshiva, and others. He studied Torah and musar for two years under Rabbi Salanter's guidance.

In 1877, Rabbi Salanter selected him to be among the first to study at the Kovna kollel.[3] In Kovna he was reunited with his wife and children, but in 1878 his wife died in childbirth. The tragic loss of his wife did not break his spirit. Indeed, it strengthened his willpower to pursue his spiritual endeavors.[4] He became an ascetic, isolating himself in a house in the courtyard of a God-fearing man named Shlomo Hapech, the tinsmith of Slobodca. He was forced to leave the house after the Maskilim informed the police that Rabbi Joseph Hurwitz "preoccupied himself with counterfeit money."[5]

After leaving his isolated quarters, Rabbi Hurwitz rejoined the group of Rabbi Salanter's disciples. He also spent much time in Kelm and Grobin with Rabbi Simhah Zissel. At this point he realized that it was not sufficient to strive for a noble character and to reach new heights in Torah study. One must also teach Torah to the masses. Toward this end he established yeshivoth, notably the one in the city of Berdichev. In his travels he met Gerson Zasinar, the proprietor of a large estate in the vicinity of Zital. Rabbi Hurwitz asked him to permit the construction of an isolated house in his forest, so that he himself might return to the ascetic life. Gerson Zasinar provided the site, and a wealthy Berliner named Lehman, who had been influenced by Rabbi Salanter's musar teachings, contributed the funds necessary for the construction of the house. Gerson Zasinar agreed to support the rabbi.

Rabbi Joseph Hurwitz lived in isolation in the forest for nine years, during which he devoted his time to Torah study, musar, and piety. At the end of the ninth year, he came out of isolation, to share his knowledge and ethical values with others.[6]

In cooperation with the followers of Rabbi Salanter, Rabbi Hurwitz was active in the establishment of kollelim for married students who excelled in Torah and piety. Such kollelim were established by Rabbi Hurwitz in the towns of Navaradock, Zital,

---

[3]Through the years a group of young disciples of Rabbi Salanter had lived in Kovna. In 1877, Rabbi Salanter raised the funds to establish a proper institution, a kollel, in which a few students, relieved of material worries, lived and studied together.

[4]See Y. L. Nekritz, op. cit., p. 248.

[5]Ibid. See also chapter: The Musar Movement and the Enlightenment.

[6]Ibid., p. 249.

Lubetz, Shavali, Dvinsk, and Lida. Each town had more than ten outstanding students studying at its kollel. The students were supported by the community and given allowances. Rabbi Hurwitz did not stay longer than a month at any of the kollelim, but during the month of Elul, students from all of the kollelim gathered in one place. At midyear, Rabbi Hurwitz invited outstanding followers of Rabbi Salanter to give musar talks to the students.[7]

The Establishment of the Navaradock Yeshiva

Rabbi Hurwitz chose Navaradock[8] as the site for the establishment of a yeshiva. At that time Rabbi Jehiel Michal Epstein was spiritual leader there, and he supported Rabbi Hurwitz in his efforts to found a yeshiva in the town. The fact that Navaradock was twenty-one miles away from a railroad was considered an asset by Rabbi Hurwitz, who favored isolating students from the outside world.[9] The Navaradock Jewish community's prominent citizens agreed to participate in the establishment of a kollel for married students and a yeshiva for single young men.[10] Rabbi Hurwitz brought to Navaradock ten outstanding students, married and single, who would serve as pillars of the yeshiva.[11]

In the beginning, the kollel and yeshiva students studied in the courtyard of the synagogue. They began at nine in the morning, took a break for lunch, and continued until time for afternoon and evening prayers, for which they gathered in a rented house. In the half-hour break between afternoon and evening prayers, musar was studied.[12]

Many generous Jews of Navaradock took on the responsibility of feeding the kollel students, who received two daily meals. The

---

[7]*Ibid.*

[8]In 1888 there were approximately five thousand inhabitants in Navaradock, which enjoyed the status of a district town. There were fifteen study houses and many distinguished rabbis. The town had a history of antiquity, having been mentioned in the Response of Rabbi Solomon Luria (1510-1573), (Response for Navaradock, No. 59, 1540). Its central synagogue was built in 1648. See *ibid.*

[9]*Ibid.*, p. 250.

[10]*Ibid.*

[11]Among these were Rabbis Meir Knisiner (last spiritual leader of Navaradock), Joseph Haim Brown (spiritual leader in the Bronx, N.Y.), Ozer Polei (of Finland and Cleveland, Ohio), Henich of Luga, Speranski of Philadelphia, Pa., Jacob Zasler (spiritual leader in Moscow who died in Israel), Haim Zelig of Zital, and others. See *Ibid.*, p. 250.

[12]*Ibid.*

meals were delivered by a porter. The students did not know the benefactors, and the benefactors did not know the students. Married students received six rubles a month for supporting their families. Unmarried yeshiva students prepared their meals in their living quarters and received three rubles a month.[13]

There was no set curriculum. Students planned their own study in a specific tractate of the Talmud and commentaries. Rabbi Hurwitz named Rabbi Elijahu bar Barkovski as masgiah (overseer) of the students in their studies and for their financial needs.

During 1896-1897, rabbis opposed to the teaching of musar in yeshivoth attacked Rabbi Hurwitz not only for this, but also for establishing kollelim. Some of these antagonists asked the communal leaders of Navaradock to withdraw financial support from the town's yeshiva and kollel.[14] Rabbi Epstein and the communal leaders responded as follows:

> Here there is no organization, no sect, no new school of thought, but Talmudic scholars engrossing themselves in the study of the Talmud and its commentaries and excelling in their studies. If the facts were contrary, we would not have supported them. We also approve of the curriculum of study, which is geared to educate outstanding scholars and righteous men. Their straight path leads them directly to the teachings of God. They shy away from money and materialistic benefits, and all their deeds are noble. We are well informed of their high standards in learning and character-building and we find that it is our duty to tell the truth to everybody.[15]

The communal leaders were also members of the board of trustees concerned with the needs of the yeshiva. The letter reveals the leaders' high opinion of the students as well as their competent administration of the yeshiva.

In another case, a rabbi demanded that funds be withdrawn from the school and Rabbi Hurwitz and his students be expelled from Navaradock. Rabbi Epstein rebuked this rabbi in the following manner:

---

[13]*Ibid.*

[14]*Ibid.*, p. 251.

[15]See letter in *Ha-Tzfira*, 1897, No. 136. See also Y. L. Nekritz, *Yeshivath Navaradock, op. cit.*, p. 251.

The lips of a man who slanders Talmudic scholars shall become speechless. Woe to the generation that indulges in spreading evil tongue. Woe to a man who occupies the chair of the rabbinate, who speaks words of heresy and atheism. . . . Such Talmudic and God-fearing scholars shall multiply among Israel and those who indulge in evil words against them shall be excommunicated.[16]

Thus Rabbi Epstein and the leaders of Navaradock stood firm behind Rabbi Hurwitz and his students during this period of controversy. After this, the Jews of Navaradock began to manifest love and understanding toward the students.[17] By 1889, the yeshiva's student body had increased to two hundred. Students came from all over Russia to study Torah and musar. His success in Navaradock inspired Rabbi Hurwitz to make plans to spread Torah and musar throughout White Russia, South Russia, and the Ukraine, since the level of Torah education there had declined.[18]

The Branching Out of the Navaradock Yeshiva

Rabbi Hurwitz's influence upon his students was powerful. His dynamic personality charmed them, his countenance exuded wisdom, and his musar talks, filled with knowledge and understanding, captivated them.[19] He was like a "well of living water" to his students. Despite his concern for the yeshiva and kollel in Navaradock, he asked his students to dedicate their lives to the establishment of yeshivoth for children, single men, and married men in other places.

Rabbi Hurwitz sought out men of means, who contributed large sums of money for the dissemination of Torah and musar. He persuaded Rabbi Zvi Gutman, spiritual leader of Tsalbus, in the district of Harson, to travel to the cities of South Russia to organize boards for the founding of new yeshivoth. He sent the outstanding students of the Navaradock kollel to head these new yeshivoth, which were established in Harson, Mohilev, Podolsk, Kamnetz-Podolsk, Berdichev, Nikolaev, Balta, and Odessa. The curriculum was oriented to the needs of three groups of students: those who were ready to study Talmud and Tosefoth with the teacher,

---

[16]See letter in *Ha-Tzfira*, 1897, No. 136. See also Y. L. Nekritz, *op. cit.*, p. 252.
[17]Y. L. Nekritz, *Ibid.*
[18]*Ibid.*
[19]*Ibid.*, p. 253.

those more advanced in such study, and those ready to study by themselves. Musar talks were part of the curriculum. Students were encouraged to continue with their studies after the completion of the course of study at the yeshiva.[20] The board of communal leaders in each city where a new yeshiva was founded assumed the financial responsibility for the yeshiva.

During the rise of the new yeshivoth, the Navaradock yeshiva became a great center of Torah learning and musar. Within twelve years of its inception it attracted such students as Rabbi Joseph Kahanaman (later Rosh Yeshiva of Poniviz), in Israel Rabbi Yehezkiel Abramsky (later of London), and many other outstanding spiritual leaders of our time.[21] With the same kind of energy that he expended on the establishment of yeshivoth for children and young men, Rabbi Hurwitz founded new kollelim in Yiveh and Shavali, White Russia.

In 1908 Rabbi Epstein, the beloved spiritual leader of Navaradock, passed away. Controversy arose over the appointment of a new rabbi, and the communal leaders of the town split into two groups. One group selected Rabbi Burstein, spiritual leader of Towrig to succeed Rabbi Epstein.

The second group opposed this choice because of Rabbi Burstein's past differences with Rabbi Epstein, and because of his antagonism toward the musar movement. Since the Navaradock Yeshiva was a center of musar teaching, Rabbi Hurwitz was naturally disturbed by this conflict. He decided to transfer two-thirds of his students to the Zital Yeshiva. Only those students who Rabbi Hurwitz was sure would not be affected by the controversy remainded in Navaradock.[22]

After six months a new rabbi was chosen, and the students returned from Zital to Navaradock, which again supported Rabbi Hurwitz and his yeshiva. Rabbi Hurwitz's interest in each individual student and his inspiring musar talks effected changes in the students' study habits and in their spiritual and ethical attitudes.[23]

---

[20]Ibid.
[21]Ibid.
[22]Ibid.
[23]Ibid. The new rabbi was Menachem Karkowsky, who agreed to support Rabbi Hurwitz and his yeshiva. However, when Rabbi Hurwitz did not permit the new spiritual leader to have a say in the matters of administrating the yeshiva, Rabbi Karkowsky opened his own school. Conflicts arose between the two, and differences continued until the First World War, which caused Rabbi Karkowsky to close down his yeshiva.

From 1910 to 1915 the Navaradock Yeshiva reached its pinnacle in Talmudic studies and in religious and ethical practices. Four separate classes heard Talmudic and musar lectures from four distinguished rabbis, Abraham Jaffan (Rabbi Hurwitz's son-in-law), Isaac Weiss (past spiritual leader of Lubatsh), Yuzpah Zvi Davidovich (writer of a book on Maimonides entitled *Imrei Joseph*), and Mordecai Steinberg (past spiritual leader of Rozsnoi).[24]

Of the students in the Navaradock Yeshiva, the following excelled in the study of Talmud and musar, and were destined to become heads of yeshivoth in the future:

Rabbi Israel Jacob Lubazanski (son-in-law of Rabbi Hurwitz and spiritual counselor of Yeshivath Ohel Torah in Baranowitz); Rabbi Abraham Zalmans (dean of the Warsaw branch of the Beth Joseph yeshivoth); Rabbi David Bliaker (dean of the Mezritz branch of Beth Joseph yeshivoth); Rabbi David Budnick (dean of the Dvinsk branch of the Beth Joseph yeshivoth); Rabbi Samuel Weintreib (spiritual leader of Karlin, and dean of the Pinsk branch of Beth Joseph yeshivoth); Rabbi Leib Hertz Smukler (academic dean of the Rozsnoi branch of the Beth Joseph yeshivoth); Rabbi Zvi Krink (member of the Yeshivath Baranowitz administration); Rabbi Fishel Schmidtzer; Rabbi Eliezer Knisiner; and Rabbi Isaac Weinstein (spiritual leader of Vishnivah and academic dean at Yeshivath Volosin in Jerusalem).[25]

In 1912 a new yeshiva building at Navaradock was completed. The first floor was a study hall for Torah and musar. On the second floor, Rabbi Hurwitz and his son-in-law, Rabbi Jaffan, lived. The study hall was also used as a place for prayer during the week and the Sabbath, and as a meeting place for all the students to hear musar talks.[26]

The outbreak of the First World War caused the Navaradock Yeshiva great economic hardship, because outside support was interrupted. Rabbi Hurwitz was forced to send some of his students to neighboring cities to collect money to keep the yeshiva going.

During the spring of 1915 a delegation arrived from Baranowitz, to ask Rabbi Hurwitz for outstanding students to strengthen the Baranowitz yeshiva. Rabbi Jaffan was dispatched forthwith,

---

[24]*Ibid.*
[25]*Ibid.*, p. 255.
[26]*Ibid.*

along with a group of excellent students, who succeeded in raising the standards of Torah learning and musar in Baranowitz.[27]

Meanwhile, the German army captured Poland and Lida, and approached the border of White Russia. Rabbi Hurwitz, fearing the detrimental impact that the Germans, with their Enlightenment, would have upon his students, decided to move the majority of them to Russia proper. (The author, in his research, inquired of a former student of Rabbi Hurwitz about the selection of students for yeshiva study. It was the rabbi's policy to open the doors to everyone, even to those not observant in the mitzvoth of the Torah and ignorant of its teachings—so long as the new students displayed a desire for learning and the will to accept change in religious observance and character-building. Rabbi Hurwitz therefore had good reason to fear the German Enlightenment, since he had students who might be easily distracted by it.) [28]

The departure from Navaradock began in the month of Elul, 1915. A small group of students remained behind to maintain the running of the school; others were forced to stay behind because of family or health reasons. Rabbi Hurwitz and his students found a new center for the Beth Joseph yeshivoth in Homel.

Beth Joseph Yeshivoth during the Homel Period

The city of Homel became a home for refugees during the First World War. It had thirty synagogues and houses of study for a Jewish population of about eighty thousand.[29] When Rabbi Hurwiz and his students arrived in town they had great difficulty finding a place to study, since most of the study houses were already filled with refugees. Finally, they were able to find a place.

The majority of the synagogues in Homel belonged to the Hasidic Jews, who used the Sephardic text for prayer. Nevertheless, the Navaradock students were graciously welcomed by the Jews of Homel. Slowly but surely Rabbi Hurwitz and his students made the necessary educational and financial readjustment in Homel. A new class for younger students, to prepare them for self-study, was instituted under the guidance of Rabbi Haim Sash, spiritual leader

---

[27]*Ibid.*

[28]Record of interview with Rabbi Isaac Orlansky, a student of Rabbi Hurwitz, October 13, 1969.

[29]See Y. L. Nekritz, *op. cit.*, p. 256.

of M'zaslah and a refugee from the war in Homel. In spite of the hard times, Rabbi Hurwitz made his yeshiva grow in quantity as well as quality.[30]

As usual, Rabbi Hurwitz was not satisfied with maintaining a yeshiva in Homel while surrounding communities lacked yeshivoth. He hoped, actually, to make Homel a center for producing outstanding students who would establish yeshivoth in other places. He decided, as was his custom in Navaradock, to send the best students to set up yeshivoth throughout the length and breadth of Russia.[31] In 1916 he sent a group of students with Rabbi Jaffan to establish a yeshiva in Rostov. Rabbi Hurwitz and his students also founded yeshivoth in the following cities in Russia: Harkov, Tsaritsan, Nishni-Bobgorod, Astrachan, Pavlograd, and Kiev. The yeshiva in Kiev became in time a center for Torah study for the surrunding towns of Dmievka, Pitoli-Krishzatik, Salaminka, Konotop, Neizhin, Preslav, Piratin, Tsirkas, and Zolotonasa. Yeshivoth were also established in Berdichev, Zhitomir, Zwil, Luvar, Korostin, Malin, Zaslov, and Old Constantinople.

Among the outstanding students of Rabbi Hurwitz in Torah and musar during the Homel period were Rabbis Israel Jacob Kanevski (Rosh Yeshiva at Bnei Brak and author of *Khiloth Jacob*), Abraham Dov Dunin (Rosh Yeshiva at the Beth Joseph branch at Titkin), and Jacob Zelden (head of Beth Joseph at Plotzk).

Other yeshivoth invited Rabbi Hurwitz to speak, to strengthen the path of Torah and musar. He spent some time in the yeshivoth of Rabbi Iser Zalman Melzer of Slutzk and Rabbi Elhanan Wasserman of Smilovitz.[32] Rabbi Hurwitz and the Navaradock school of musar influenced youth in general and yeshiva students in particular.[33]

During this period Rabbi Melzer was asked why Rabbi Hurwitz had published so few books and articles. Rabbi Melzer answered that his faith and dedication were his publications.[34] As the Beth Joseph yeshivoth continued to increase in number, it became necessary to call a conference in Homel of all of Rabbi Hurwitz's

[30]*Ibid.*
[31]*Ibid.*
[32]*Ibid.*, p. 256f.
[33]*Ibid.*, p. 257.
[34]*Ibid.*, p. 258.

students, so that they might hear his thoughts and be motivated by his dynamic personality.

Students from the various yeshivoth in Homel gathered to hear him speak. His thoughts later appeared in *Madregath ha-Adam* (*Man's Standard*). He expressed his views on man's standards from the time of creation until his own day. He traced the history of man through the epochs of Adam, Noah, Abraham, Mount Sinai, the Prophets, and the epoch of Talmud and yeshivoth.

The Epoch of Adam

Before the sin, Adam's mind was not influenced by extrinsic and natural forces. His willpower and nature were not strong enough to pervert his judgment in choosing evil over good. He recognized evil and resisted it in order to do good. Adam's understanding was like that of an angel and his body was similar to a garment. Adam and Eve were not ashamed of their nakedness because their bodies were like eternal garments, which never needed removal.

In only one way did Adam differ from an angel: he had the choice between the life of an angel or the life of a man, which depended upon his eating from the "tree of knowledge." After Adam ate from this tree, his emotions and passions were aroused to compete with his understanding in his future decisions concerning evil and good, truth and falsehood, and the world of the spirit vis-à-vis the world of materialism.[35]

The Epoch of Noah and the Flood Generation

From Adam, there began a new epoch in the spiritual way of life in man. From now on, man's mental and spiritual ways would compete with his physical and psychological ones, until the former or the latter would win out in the struggle. After Adam, people failed to resist these latter temptations, until wickedness became the order of the day, wickedness that affected even the animals, so that God decided to destroy His creation.

Noah alone was able to withstand the evil of his generation. He served God with all his strength and ability, needing help, however, in matters concerning love and fear of God. According to Rabbi Hurwitz, the Sages in the Talmud did not question Noah's

---

[35]See Rabbi Hurwitz, *Madregath ha-Adam* (Jerusalem, 1964), I, pp. 2, 4f.

righteousness, or argue about Noah's standards of righteousness compared to Abraham's. Instead, they asked the questions, why was Noah such a righteous man, and what caused him to be one?

One held that Noah's search for the truth enabled him to rise above his generation's wickedness, and that surely if he had lived in Abraham's time he would have been a more righteous man, because he would not have had to contend with such evil. Another held that Noah's search for truth was not enough to make him rise above others of his time, but that he realized that he must strive for perfection. Perhaps, had Noah lived in Abraham's time he would not have so striven for perfection, since that generation was more righteous and thus less threatening to the spiritual and moral ways of life.[36]

The Epoch of Abraham

After the passing of ten generations characterized by obliviousness to God and His teachings, there appeared Abraham, who brought the world once more to the belief in one God. His relatives and others of his generation could not parallel his searching mind. His faith in God reached such heights that he was able to resist the temptations of Satan. He was master over evil and needed no help in loving and fearing God.

The Epoch of Mount Sinai

Although Abraham was able to check the power of evil, he did not succeed in achieving the standard of Adam prior to his sin. He was not in complete control over his emotions (witness his tears at the time of taking the knife to slaughter Isaac). The sensual passions which the serpent inculcated in Adam and Eve did not cease in mankind until the giving of the Torah at Mount Sinai. There, the Jews reached once more the standard of Adam prior to his sin, when they said, "We will do and we will listen." They decided to live according to the commands of God, without demanding compromises and without hesitation over whether to receive or not receive the Torah. Jethro's advice to Moses, to appoint judges to judge and to teach the laws of the Torah, resulted in the study of

---

[36]Ibid., pp. 5, 6, 7.

Torah between an individual and his friend, which continued until the period of the Prophets.[37]

The Epoch of the Prophets

Moses in his time judged the Israelites and taught them the Torah. Such was also the method of the prophets, who, according to the Gaon of Vilna, used to tell each person his fault and its correction. The generations of the prophets, however, were far different from that of Moses, when all Jews felt the spirit of the Torah and wanted to be educated in its ways by Moses and his assistants. In the generations of the prophets there were Jews who lacked such a commitment and who were even known to say, "Crazy is the prophet." Others of course were eager to be instructed in the ways of God, and the prophets were successful in leading these to the search for truth.

This is well-illustrated by Elijah's challenge to the false prophets. Elijah, by his conviction and sincere feeling for truth, was able to bring the worshipers of Baal back to the ways of the Torah.

After the prophet Malachi, the era of the prophets came to an end, and the epoch of yeshivoth began.

The Epoch of Yeshivoth

The world of the Talmud and yeshivoth opened new "wells of living water." The Yeshivoth of Sura and Pumbeditha raised the spiritual life of the Jews throughout the Diaspora. Jews realized that the source of truth lay in the yeshiva, that without it everything was meaningless. The masses began to look upon the yeshiva as a watchtower of truth and faith in God and His Torah.[38]

The yeshiva in its heyday produced people who excelled in their faith in God, in character, in the study of Torah, and in good deeds. When they left the yeshivoth for the "outside world" they set an example in sanctification of God and served as models for the wholeness of man. The yeshiva provided the world with outstanding men who spread Torah and wisdom to the masses. The outside world in these times was closely affiliated with the yeshivoth, thus the yeshiva student found it unnecessary to worry about temptations from it.

---

[37]Ibid., p. 6f.
[38]Ibid.

However, with the advent of the "cursed Haskalah," which led many astray to the point of despising the word of God, an end came to the flourishing of the yeshivoth. Many yeshiva students, feeling that there could be no compromise between the yeshiva world and the outside world, went over to the Haskalah movement. Students who stayed in the yeshivoth also became infected by the ideas of the Haskalah, compromising between the good (as represented by the yeshivoth) and the evil (as represented by the Haskalah). Since there can be no such compromise, such students were led astray.

To save the yeshivoth, then, it was necessary to bind the yeshiva world with the outside world through the education of spiritual giants. It was possible, Rabbi Hurwitz felt, to unite both worlds by raising the standards of the yeshivoth and sending out into the world men dedicated to God, Torah, and the cause of rebuilding the outside world to harmony with Torah.[39] Rabbi Hurwitz spoke to his students as follows:

> If we sincerely want to reach spiritual heights once more, and if, indeed, the ways of the Torah are precious in our eyes, we must have no fear that we would fail in our mission. We must only try, we must dedicate ourselves . . . and God will help us to carry out our plans for fulfilling the verse "You shall make me a Holy Temple and I shall dwell among you."[40]

Improvement of Character

His disciples collected all his musar talks in twelve brochures entitled *Madregath ha-Adam,* with subtitles such as "Improvement of Character"; "Ways of Repentance"; "Ways of Reliance." These talks, held by Rabbi Hurwitz before his students on various occasions, contained his theory of musar.

The sages compare the righteous to a lofty mountain, the wicked to a single hair. A person becomes wicked after being enticed by Satan to transgress the commands of the Torah step by step —a "single-hair" process. If Satan tempted man to renounce the Torah all at once, man would not listen, for he would then understand that his future path would be one of suffering and evil. The

---

[39]*Ibid.*
[40]*Ibid.*

righteous man's insight into the Satanic process causes him to fear it and to guard himself against it with all his strength. The wicked man, who lacks this insight, reasons, how can the "single-hair" process of Satan do him harm? He therefore commits one sin after another, until he confronts the wickedness of his deeds, which now appear to him as big as a mountain. The wicked man, trapped, cannot renounce his evil ways, and dies a sinner.[41]

Improvement of character, according to Rabbi Hurwitz, could be achieved through checking the evil traits of jealousy and lasciviousness. The study of Torah and the keeping of its commands are an effective means of improving character. Torah, for man, is like a bridge of steel. Man, taught Rabbi Hurwitz, must receive the teaching of the Torah through the will power of *doing* before *listening*, and must be confident that the ways of the Torah would not harm him but would help him to achieve character and security.[42]

Ways of Repentance

In matters dealing with money and sickness, people are meticulously careful to avoid making mistakes (as in counting money and taking temperature). However, in matters of self-perfection, man cannot avoid making mistakes in reckoning his good and bad deeds. Mistakes in counting money and reading a temperature may cause a temporary loss, to be sure, but mistakes in matters of self-perfection may cause a permanent loss, and so they should be avoided all the more.[43]

Since man does not, then, have a tendency to make mistakes in matters of money and sickness, he tries for perfection in these areas. He does, however, tend to make mistakes in counting his good and bad deeds.[44] Man must rely on the Torah to guide him in the correction of his bad deeds, since the Torah alone is the judge of what is good. Man has the ability to repent evil deeds and change for the good in the matter of a minute. If man would not change in a minute, he would not change forever. He must decide in the space

---

[41]Joseph Yozel Hurwitz, "Tikun ha-Midoth" in *Madregath ha-Adam, Ibid.,* p. 28f.

[42]*Ibid.,* p. 34.

[43]See Rabbi Hurwitz, "Darchei ha-Tsuvah" in *Madregath ha-Adam, Ibid.,* p. 132f.

[44]*Ibid.,* p. 146f.

of a minute to change for the good and to follow the commands of the Torah.[45]

An example of this can be a person who works in his store on the Sabbath and wants to repent. He says that he will close his store for one hour and then for two hours on the Sabbath. However, the closing of the store for an hour or two will never take place. If it does not cause this man pain to have the store open all day, then he would not bother to close it for several hours.[46]

Ways of Reliance

When man repents and returns to God, he must find his reliance in God rather than in man. The prophet Jeremiah said, "Thus saith the Lord: Cursed is the man that trusts in man and makes flesh his arm, and whose heart departs from the Lord. For he shall be like a tamarisk in the desert. . . . Blessed is the man that trusts in the Lord, and whose trust the Lord is. For he shall be as a tree planted by the waters."[47] Reliance in God serves a double purpose. It provides peace of mind from worries and anxieties, for the person has faith that God will help tomorrow as he did yesterday. It also enables man to feel more secure in times of adversity: danger, war, and other vicissitudes of life.[48] Reliance in God is one of the paramount fundamentals of the Torah. If man commits himself wholeheartedly to trust in God, then the Lord will be his helper.[49]

Contemporary School of Thought

Rabbi Hurwitz's times were marked by the Haskalah movement, the rise of the Socialist Bund, Zionism, and Communism.[50] He realized that in order to inspire young people to Torah and ethical behavior he must produce a new school of thought, one that would educate a generation of youth to have the will, the conviction, and the courage to resist philosophies and ideologies contrary to the teachings of the Torah. He felt that it was useless to wage war with the Haskalah. Rather, he believed that one must devote

[45]Ibid., p. 151.
[46]Ibid., p. 152.
[47]See Jeremiah, 17:5-7.
[48]Rabbi Hurwitz, "Darchei ha-Bitahon" in *Madregath ha-Adam, Ibid.,* p. 182.
[49]Ibid., p. 255.
[50]See chapter: *The Times of the Musar Movement.*

one's time and energy to building yeshivoth, to educating thousands of students, and to cultivating God-fearing, ethical leaders who would guide the average Jew in the ways of Torah and musar.

The Kelm and the Navaradock schools of thought are at opposite poles in the Musar Movement. The former sought to make peace between religion and general knowledge, while the latter aimed at separating the two. In Kelm, Rabbi Simhah Zissel stressed order, meticulous cleanliness and appearance. In Navaradock a student was judged not by appearance but by inner discipline. The Kelm and the Navaradock schools shared a common goal, that of the improvement of man through musar, but their methods differed totally one from the other.

Curriculum of the Navaradock School

The curriculum of the Navaradock chain of yeshivoth consisted of the daily study of musar, daily study of the *Shulhan Arukh, Orah Hayyim,* the portion of the week and the study of the same tractate of the Talmud in all the yeshivoth. Students studied with partners. Secular subjects were left out of the curriculum. There were classes from 10 a.m. until 3 p.m., then a half hour of musar study, then the afternoon prayer. Classes resumed from 5 to 9 p.m., followed by a half hour of musar study, the evening prayer, and a half hour discussion of the students' progress in learning and ethical behavior that day.[51]

The curriculum emphasized extreme positions. Neutrality was rejected. Said Rabbi Hurwitz: "I believe that in spiritual matters one can be either warm or cold, not lukewarm." The purpose of the curriculum was to inculcate in each student love for the study of Torah, true religiousness, yir'at shamayim, and achieving self-control before attempting to guide or control others. Rabbi Hurwitz held that only a man who was capable of complete self-control was qualified to become a leader in the community.[52]

One of the important characteristics of the curriculum was to instill in the students extreme ecstasy. During holidays, this ecstasy would take a happy form, but on solemn occasions, such as the High Holidays, the students appeared anxious and troubled.[53]

---

[51]Y. L. Nekritz, *Yeshivath Navaradock, op. cit.,* p. 281.

[52]See *Madregath ha-Adam, op. cit.,* pp. 58-59.

[53]See Hayyim Zaichyk, *Ha-M'orot Hagdolim* (Jerusalem: Israeli Publication Committee, 1962) pp. 156-158.

The "Boerse" ("Stock exchange") was a form of discussion in which small groups of students, sometimes pairs of them, discussed their personal problems and jointly sought methods of self-improvement. These exchange discussions exerted a profound influence on the students and helped them develop lifelong friendships. Rabbi Hurwitz, in keeping with the teachings of Rabbi Salanter, would not permit his students to rely completely on these group sessions, holding, instead, that a student of musar must strike a balance between individual and group life. Therefore he and his students made solitary retreats, known as hit'bod'dut, for musar study and reflection.[54]

The Navaradock School after Rabbi Hurwitz's Death

After Rabbi Hurwitz's death in 1919 no changes were made in the curriculum of the Navaradock Yeshivoth. From 1919 to 1968 Rabbi Abraham Jaffan, the son-in-law of Rabbi Hurwitz, headed the Navaradock Yeshivoth in Russia, Poland, America and Israel respectively. Before the Second World War, he headed a chain of sixty yeshivoth and four thousand students in Poland.[55]

Rabbi Jaffan was a courageous Rosh Yeshiva who kept the doors of the yeshivoth open even under Communism.[56] When the Communists started a reign of terror against yeshivoth, Rabbi Jaffan and his students fled to Poland, where they stayed from 1921 until 1923. It was in Poland that the Navaradock yeshivoth became known as the Beth Joseph Yeshivoth, in memory of the founder, Rabbi Hurwitz. The chain of Beth Joseph Yeshivoth made a profound impact on Polish Jewry, educating thousands of students who in turn became spiritual leaders, roshei yeshivoth, communal leaders, and businessmen, who kept the flame of Torah burning and who practiced the musar teachings of Rabbi Hurwitz under the most difficult conditions.

Rabbi Jaffan managed to escape the atrocities awaiting European Jewry in the Second World War, arriving in New York in 1942. In America he founded the Beth Joseph Yeshiva in Brooklyn, which is headed at the present time by his son, Rabbi Jacob Jaffan, and his son-in-law, Rabbi Yehuda Leib Nekritz.

---

[54]*Ibid.*, p. 160.
[55]Y. L. Nekritz, *Yeshivath Navaradock, op. cit.*, p. 274.
[56]See chapter: *The Musar Movement and the Bolsheviks.*

The entire chain of Beth Joseph Yeshivoth in Europe was destroyed in the Second World War. Thousands of students, followers of the Navaradock school of musar, were killed. Although the school established a branch in Tel Aviv in 1929 and a new center in Brooklyn, its influence on American and Israeli Jewry since the Second World War has been local, rather than national, in scope. Its influence is limited to the surviving students and followers of Rabbi Hurwitz and Rabbi Jaffan. Its yeshiva in Brooklyn does not have the prestige enjoyed by such Talmudic centers as Lakewood, Telshe, and Mirer. However, it is the opinion of the author that the Navaradock school of musar has relevancy for those who seek ethical values, self-discipline, dedication, and courage. Indeed, many of our Jewish youth today would find purpose here, because it is against middle-class values. The author was moved to tears by the musar talks of the late Rabbi Jaffan, and was inspired personally by his great learning, piety and courage.

The Literature of the Navaradock School of Thought

Rabbi Hurwitz left many articles revealing his thought and attitudes toward the religious, educational, moral, and social conditions of his time. In 1964, *Madregath ha-Adam,* which contains articles dealing with musar, God-fearing, education, self-analysis, self-recognition, and good traits based upon the Torah, was published. This work is indispensable as primary source material.

One can also find many of the rabbi's articles in *Sefer Or ha-Musar,* Volumes I and II, published in 1965 and 1966 by the Navaradock Yeshivoth. Rabbi Y. L. Nekritz's article in the Yeshivath Navaradock is of great importance as a primary source. Dov Katz's *Tenuath ha-Musar,* Volume IV, is an excellent primary source, since the author had personal access to the manuscripts of Rabbi Hurwitz and to those of his contemporaries. Finally, in 1970 Rabbi Hurwitz's article "To Turn the Many to Righteousness" was translated into English by Shraga Silverstein.

The article on Rabbi Hurwitz by Joshua Levin in *Ha-Meliz* (1883) is essential for the study of the origin of the Navaradock school of musar.

There follows a sample of one of Rabbi Hurwitz's articles, intended to show primary source as well as its value for our time.

To Turn the Many to Righteousness

Just as when one recognizes a shortcoming within himself, he is impelled, according to the extent of his recognition, to seek means toward its correction, and undertakes all manner of exertion toward the desired end, pursuing it unremittingly, so—and how much more so—when one becomes aware of as grievous a failing within society as its present educational structure, which has taken such tremendous toll of our youth—how much more so must he summon up all of his powers to guard the breach, remove the impediment, and raise up the standard of truth. This is especially true in our days, when the nets of the doctrine of sin are cast even over the very young, when all the paths of Torah are desolate, and when there remain but a chosen few who stand steadfast and unflinching upon their watch. But "where there are no kids, there are no goats." If the present state of affairs is permitted to persist, there is a danger (God forbid) that in the course of time Torah will vanish from Israel. This being so, there is no alternative but to rouse ourselves from our slumber, take cognizance of the dangers which confront us and do battle with them, with all of our talents and sensitivities, with all of the means at our disposal.

But who is more keenly aware of the absence of Torah and fear of God than those who meditate in God's Law day and night, those who are sensitive to the meaning of perfection, and, consequently, to the spuriousness and deceptiveness of an educational system which holds uncontested sway? Upon them devolves the duty of doing all within their power in this province. They must not seek to exempt themselves by any form or manner of excuse, and they must not look jealously upon their time and upon their own efforts at self-improvement—for the spiritual life of their people is at stake.

In view of the fact, however, that their lack of familiarity with the underlying bases and the various ramifications of this particular aspect of Divine service leads them to seek rationalizations for its evasion, it becomes necessary to consider it, so that such evasion will come to be seen as entirely inadmissible. . . .[57]

The wonder grows when we consider that Rabbi Chiyya, the compiler of the baraisot, the foundations of the Talmud, gave all his education in the service of the community, beginning with those who had barely entered "the Lord's vineyard"—the four ells of halakha and fear of God. It is clear, then, that he regarded such education as essential even for those of so tender an age. . . .[58]

[57]Rabbi Hurwitz, *To Turn the Many to Righteousness*, translated by Shraga Silverstein (Jerusalem, 1970), pp. 9-13.
[58]*Ibid*, p. 21.

CHAPTER 12

THE SLOBODCA SCHOOL OF MUSAR AND ITS FOUNDER, RABBI NATHAN ZVI FINKEL

Rabbi Nathan (Note) Zvi Hirsch Finkel, the son of Rabbi Moses Finkel, was born in the town of Rossein in Lithuania. Orphaned at an early age, he was cared for by an uncle in Vilna. Very little is known of his childhood and adolescence, since all of his life he refused to talk about himself.

At the age of fifteen he was already known as a Talmudic scholar. He married the granddaughter of Rabbi Eliezer Gutman,[1] then spiritual leader of Kelm. Living in Kelm after his marriage, he was influenced by the musar talks of Rabbi Simhah Zissel.[2]

During his stay in Kelm, Rabbi Finkel assisted Rabbi Simhah Zissel in the administration of the famous Beth Hatalmud. He impressed Rabbi Simhah Zissel with his pedagogical and administrative skills. He gathered students to the school and succeeded in influencing them to adopt the musar teachings of Rabbi Simhah Zissel.

In 1876, after the Beth Hatalmud closed down,[3] Rabbi Simhah Zissel made Rabbi Finkel his assistant at the yeshiva in Grobin. Since the two did not always agree on matters of education and musar, Rabbi Finkel left Grobin to start his own musar yeshiva.

The Establishment of the Slobodca Kollel

Rabbi Finkel saw that the standards of Torah study in his time, low to begin with, were continuing to decline because, in spite of the many students engrossed in the study of Torah, there prevailed a lack of guidance and purpose, as well as facilities for students who wished to pursue postgraduate studies.[4]

---

[1]For more information on Rabbi Gutman and his family, who traced their descent to King David, see E. E. Friedman, *Sefer ha-Zichronoth 1858-1926* (Tel Aviv, 1926), pp. 8-40.

[2]Interview with Rabbi Jacob M. Lesin, a student of Rabbi Finkel from 1903-1912, August 28, 1970. See also Dov Katz, *Tenuath ha-Musar*, III, 18f.

[3]See chapter dealing with Rabbi Simhah Zissel for reasons of this closing.

[4]Interview with Rabbi Lesin, *op. cit.* See also Dov Katz, *op. cit.*, III, 20.

In 1877-1878 the first yeshiva, a kollel for married students, was established in Slobodca. Rabbi Finkel and Rabbi Eliezer Jacob obtained the support of Lachman, a wealthy Berlin Jew, who donated ten thousand marks to the kollel.[5] Lachman not only made this initial contribution to the kollel, but continued to support musar institutions morally as well as financially.

Rabbi Jacob selected ten married students for the Slobodca kollel,[6] among them Rabbi Eliezer Sulbitz of Lomza, Rabbi Isaac Meltzen, Rabbi Naphtali Hertz Halevi, Rabbi Zvi Hirsh, Rabbi Note Ginzburg, and Rabbi Naphtali Amsterdam. Rabbi Amsterdam wrote the following impression of the kollel in Slobodca:

> The outstanding ascetic Torah scholars made the kollel a tree of life and a precious corner. From there they are destined to come out as outstanding teachers to serve the Jewish people and to set a model for high achievement in Torah study and God-fearing. From there they will come out well prepared to assume the responsibilities of the Rabbinate in the largest Jewish communities. They are engrossed in their studies diligently, and are supported by philanthropists, lovers of Torah.[7]

Eliezer E. Friedman wrote his impressions:

> When I arrived at Slobodca, I decided to continue with my studies at the kollel. I entered the house of study in the late afternoon and I found the young married men wrapped in the phylacteries and shawl, and they were pacing the floor back and forth. One of them sings a sad tune . . . another has his face glued to the book *Rashith Hokhma* and mumbles silently. . . . They communicate with each other, through hints, and fragmentary Hebrew words. . . . Others do not talk at all and use the eyes and hands to make their needs known. . . . They are ascetic. I decided to go to Kovna to study in the Beth Midrash of Joseph Rabinowitz. . . .[8]

---

[5]See E. E. Friedman, "Toldoth Baalei ha-Musar" in *Ha-Meliz*, No. 115, 1897. See also Friedman, *Sefer ha-Zichronoth, op. cit.*, p. 131.

[6]*Ibid.*

[7]See Rabbi Naphtali Amsterdam's article on the Slobodca kollel in *Ha-Lebanon*, 1879, p. 36.

[8]See E. E. Friedman, *Sefer ha-Zichronoth, op. cit.*, p. 131.

According to Friedman, the *musarniks* of Kelm were responsible for influencing married students toward musar and asceticism
at the expense of Talmud.[9] It is important at this point to include
Friedman's impression of Torah study by married students in
Kovna because it influenced to a great extent Friedman's decision
to campaign against financial support for the Slobodca kollel. He
wrote as follows:

> After I settled in my new house of study, I visited young
> men who are scattered throughout the houses of study in
> Kovna. I found them to be outstanding young men of the
> Jewish people, who manifest sagacity and expertise in Tal-
> mudic literature. There are among them those who are
> fluent in both the Jerusalem and the Babylonian Talmud
> —like Rabbi Mendel ha-Yorburgi—true geniuses. They
> study diligently and make remarkable progress. However,
> their economic condition is miserable. There is no one who
> pays any attention to their adversity. There are those con-
> templating leaving behind their studies in order to earn a
> living for their families, because they receive letters filled
> with tears over the poverty at home. . . . They are the ones
> who truly fulfill the aspirations of Lachman and are fit to
> study in the kollel in Slobodca in place of those as-
> cetics. . . .[10]

E. E. Friedman decided to undertake a propaganda campaign
against the kollel in Slobodca. He consulted Rabbi Meshel of Alik-
sut, who was sympathetic to the hardships suffered by the young
men of Kovna and antagonistic toward the Slobodca kollel. The two
joined forces, and a committee headed by Rabbi Meshel pleaded
their cause before Rabbi Isaac Elhanan Spektor. The latter, willing to identify with the cause, nevertheless hesitated to do anything
without first calling a conference of Rabbis to discuss and make a
decision concerning this matter.[11]

To this conference came such notables as Rabbi Salanter, Rabbi Alexander Moses Lapidus, Rabbi Benison, the spiritual leader

---

[9]*Ibid.*
[10]*Ibid.*, p. 131f.
[11]*Ibid.*, p. 132.

of Calabria, and others.[12] The conference reported its decision as follows:

> The kollel of Slobodca is not fulfilling the purpose for which it was established by its benefactor . . . On the other hand, those in Kovna fulfill the requirements of the Slobodca institution and merit special attention. In order to avoid a controversy among the Jews by seizing control of the Slobodca institution, it has been decided not to interfere in matters concerning the Slobodca kollel, but rather to organize a committee to raise the necessary funds for the support of worthy young men, dedicated to Talmudic scholarship and fit to serve Jewish communities as future rabbis, until rabbinical posts are found for them, so that they will not be forced to abandon Torah study until they have achieved their purpose.[13]

The conference was responsible, then, for founding an organization for seeing to the financial welfare of the Kovna students and their families.[14] It was called "Organization for the support of ascetic young men in Kovna." The organization also undertook the expansion of kollelim in other cities, and to encourage financial assistance for them. Friedman was given the public relations job and was responsible for editing the bulletins which were signed by both Rabbi Salanter and Rabbi Isaac Elhanan. Messengers carried these bulletins to many parts of Russia, and in a short period of time new kollelim emerged in the cities of such districts as Kovna, Vilna, Minsk, and elsewhere. Thus outstanding scholars were permitted to continue their Talmudic studies, unhampered by constant concern for their families' financial welfare, until they were called to rabbinical posts.[15]

During the time that Rabbi Finkel worked in behalf of the Slobodca and the Kovna kollelim, he also served as masgiah in the Yeshiva Orah Hayyim, which had been established for elementary-school children by Rabbi Zvi Levitan. Rabbi Finkel made changes in the school, adding classes, improving the financial condition, ex-

---

[12]*Ibid.*
[13]*Ibid.*, p. 132f.
[14]*Ibid.*, p. 133.
[15]*Ibid.*

pelling unfit students, appointing another rosh yeshiva, Rabbi Shlomo Note Kotler, and constructing a new building. His most important contribution, however, was his devotion to raising the morals and learning standards of the students. He took an interest in each student. He lectured on musar. His musar talks made a strong impression on these students, especially in matters of faith and God-fearing.[16]

In 1878, Rabbi Finkel established a yeshiva for outstanding Talmudic students in the study house Halvaith Hamath.

In the early years of Halvaith Hamath, Rabbi Isaac Blazer and Rabbi Abraham Shenker lectured in Talmud and delivered musar talks to the students. The students also came into contact with the men of the Slobodca kollel, who inspired them to emulate their example in wisdom and musar.[17]

The Establishment of the Slobodca Yeshiva

In 1882, Rabbi Finkel established the Slobodca Yeshiva in the old Slobodca study house. The graduates of the elementary school Orah Hayyim were his first students. Additional students came from the many cities of Lida. Rabbi Finkel poured all his skill and energy into the Slobodca Yeshiva, which over a period of fifty years spread Torah and musar throughout Jewish communities in Europe, America, and Israel.[18] The yeshiva reflected Rabbi Finkel's personality and his ideas and ideals concerning Judaism and musar.[19]

In the beginning, Rabbi Finkel did not appoint roshei yeshivoth to lecture to the students. Instead, he relied on the kollel students for discussions and casuistic arguments on halakha. Every now and then Rabbi Blazer and Rabbi Eliezer Gordon were invited to lecture.

In 1886, Rabbi Hayyim Rabinowitz was appointed rosh yeshiva on a full-time basis. He was considered one of the most outstanding roshei yeshivoth of his time, and as such attracted gifted students to study under him.[20]

---

[16]Interview with Rabbi Lesin, *op. cit.*, verified by Rabbi Joseph Zvi Halevi, a student at Yeshiva Orah Hayyim in 1883. See Dov Katz, *Tenuath ha-Musar, op. cit.*, III, 27.

[17]See Rabbi Naphtali Amsterdam's remarks in Dov Katz, *Tenuath ha-Musar, op. cit.*, III, 27.

[18]Interview with Rabbi Lesin, *op. cit.* See also *Tenuath ha-Musar, op. cit.*, III, 31.

[19]Interview with Rabbi Lesin, *op. cit.*

[20]*Ibid.*

After several years, Rabbi Finkel chose Rabbi Abraham Aaron Burstein to lecture to the older students and to guide those engaged in the study of Responsa literature. Then, after Rabbi Hayyim Rabinowitz and Rabbi Burstein left the Slobodca Yeshiva, Rabbi Isaac Rabinowitz replaced them in 1890 as Rosh Yeshiva.

Rabbi Isaac Rabinowitz

When Rabbi Isaac Rabinowitz, who was also known as Itzele of Poniviez, became Rosh Yeshiva in Slobodca, he played an important role in the development of the method of learning there.[21] He discouraged casuistic, hairsplitting arguments in the study of Talmud, and emphasized thinking and understanding rather than memorization. Both he and Rabbi Hayyim Soloveitchik revolutionized the method of Talmud study by placing emphasis on understanding a Talmudic topic so well that in the end a student would be able to dissect the topic into many parts in order to bring forth its essence. Both rabbis also advocated quality rather than quantity in the study of Talmud. They felt it was possible to become an outstanding Talmudist by understanding and knowing lucidly only one tractate of the Talmud, while one could study the whole Talmud and remain an ignoramus if the learning was not done intelligently.[22]

Students began to flock to the Slobodca Yeshiva when Rabbi Itzele's approach to Talmud study became known. When the Volosin Yeshiva closed in 1902, many of its students discovered that the standards of Talmud study at the Slobodca Yeshiva were just as high as they had been in the yeshiva at Volosin.[23]

The Teaching of Musar in Slobodca

In addition to Rabbi Itzele's new approach to the study of Talmud, Rabbi Finkel introduced the study of musar and pedagogical principles and methods in guiding the individual student.

Rabbi Finkel possessed unusual abilities in guiding the individual student. He was blessed in having the combined qualities of the expert psychologist and the master teacher. He knew each student intimately and always sought to get to the core of his char-

---

[21]Interview with Rabbi Lesin, op. cit.
[22]Ibid.
[23]Ibid. See also Dov Katz, Tenuath ha-Musar, op. cit., III, 32.

acter. He judged the behavior, personality and character of a student on the basis of observations and numerous talks with him. He would converse with a student about his home background and other such nonschool matters, holding that such talks revealed a student's attitudes and character more than scholarly discussions did.[24]

Rabbi Finkel rebuked his students for seemingly small offenses in good manners and appearance. He was convinced that major offenses were the result of a series of smaller ones, and that therefore it was a "must" to overcome insignificant failings before they developed into behavior patterns. For example, in stressing the importance of proper care of one's clothes, he used to say: "A wrinkled or shapeless hat is indicative of a disorganized mind."[25]

He felt it necessary to create a relaxed and happy atmosphere in the yeshiva, as a prerequisite to study and creativity.[26] Although Rabbi Finkel showed concern for all his students, he nevertheless saw to it that the brilliant ones were favored, and so guided that they could realize their greatness in Torah study, musar, and communal leadership.[27]

Rabbis Dov Zvi Heller, Moshe Mordecai Epstein and Iser Zalman Meltzer

In 1890, Rabbi Finkel named Rabbi Dov Zvi Heller as masgiah of the yeshiva. He was a very righteous man, seldom seen outside the walls of the yeshiva. He was in charge of the schedule of study and dean of students, supervising student behavior. He took an intimate interest in every student and passed on his detailed observations to Rabbi Finkel. He was consulted in matters of policy and problem-solving. He eased Rabbi Finkel's burden by assuming the responsibility for the students' housing and board. In his early years at the yeshiva Rabbi Heller was responsible for delivering musar talks before groups of students.[28] In 1934, he settled in Palestine, and he died there in 1936. He was succeeded by Rabbi Dov Zowchowski.

[24]Interview with Rabbi Lesin, op. cit.
[25]Ibid.
[26]Ibid.
[27]Ibid.
[28]Ibid. See also Rabbi Ephraim Ashri, "Yeshivoth Kneseth Israel in Slobodca" in Mirsky's Mosdoth Torah b'Europa b'Binyanim u b'Hurbanam, p. 146f. See also Dov Katz, Tenuath ha-Musar, op. cit., p. 3.

When Rabbi Isaac Rabinowitz left Slobodca in 1894 to become spiritual leader of Grozed, he was replaced by Rabbi Finkel's two brothers-in-law, Rabbi Moshe Mordecai Epstein and Rabbi Iser Zalman Meltzer. Both delivered Talmudic lectures to the students once a week, Rabbi Epstein on Monday and Rabbi Meltzer on Thursday.

Rabbi Meltzer was born in the city of Mir in 1870 and died in Jerusalem in 1954. He studied in the yeshivoth of Volosin and Radun, and stayed in Slobodca for three years, accepting, in 1897, the position of spiritual leader of Slutzk. There, with a nucleus of several of Rabbi Finkel's outstanding students, he started the Slutzk Yeshiva. In 1928 he settled in Jerusalem, where he became head of the Yeshiva Etz Hayyim. He left behind writings on Maimonides, known as *Eben ha-Ezel*.[29]

With the departure of Rabbi Meltzer to Slutzk in 1897, Rabbi Epstein remained the sole Rosh Yeshiva in Slobodca. Rabbi Epstein was born in 1866 in the city of Bakst in Lida and died in 1934 in Jerusalem. A student of the Volosin and Radun yeshivoth, he was appointed spiritual leader of the Slobodca Jewish community in 1912.

As a rosh yeshiva, Rabbi Epstein assumed the financial and educational responsibilities of the yeshiva. His Talmudic lectures were based on Rabbi Hayyim Brisker's method, which stressed a logical approach to the study of Talmud.[30] He also found time to write his well-known book *Lwush Mordecai* on the Talmud tractate Baba Kama, and to write responses to any halakhic inquiries.

His love for and dedication to the yeshiva knew no bounds; he placed it above his own personal material betterment. When the communal leaders of Bialystok urged him to accept the rabbinate there and offered him a high salary, he refused the offer. He told them, "How can I leave the holy Yeshiva for my personal material betterment? How can I live without it?"[31]

The Revolt against Musar in Slobodca

A major revolt against the teaching of musar took place in the Slobodca Yeshiva in 1897. Rebellious students organized to abolish

---

[29]Interview with Rabbi Lesin, *op. cit.* See also Ephraim Ashri, *op. cit.*, p. 145.
[30]Interview with Rabbi Lesin, *op. cit.*
[31]*Ibid.*, See also Rabbi Ashri, *op. cit.*

the study of musar, and caused a split in the student body. Both sides were invited to a Rabbinical Court in Kovna. The majority of rabbis on this court were critics of the Musar Movement, therefore a verdict was handed down in favor of the dissenters.[32]

After this, Rabbi Isaac Blazer came forward with an announcement in *Ha-Meliz* that he would publish, in the future, a book concerning the views of outstanding rabbis on the study of musar in Slobodca and other institutions.[33] In 1900 his book, *Or Israel,* appeared as an answer to the critics of musar.

Rabbi Finkel and his loyal students—sixty out of three hundred—left the Slobodca Yeshiva, to start another institution where musar could be taught. The dissenting students took over the financial matters of the yeshiva, and continued to spread propaganda against Rabbi Finkel in the community.

Rabbi Epstein and Rabbi Heller left Slobodca with Rabbi Finkel. The new heads of the Slobodca Yeshiva offered Rabbi Epstein a high salary to stay on, but he said that he would "go with the truth, and the truth is with Rabbi Finkel."[34]

And so Rabbi Finkel set up a new yeshiva with his loyal students. The rebellious students remained in the Slobodca Yeshiva, which became known as Kneseth Beth Itzhak, named after Rabbi Isaac Elhanan. Rabbi Finkel's new yeshiva was named Kneseth Israel, in honor of Rabbi Israel Salanter.

The Kneseth Beth Itzhak was headed by Rabbi Moses Danishewski, spiritual leader of Slobodca, and Rabbi Zvi Rabinowitz, spiritual leader of Kovna. Both were actively engaged in opposing musar at this time.

Contemporary School of Thought

The times of Rabbi Finkel were shaped by the influence of the Haskalah, which as we have seen advocated change in accordance to the ideals of the Enlightenment. Rabbi Finkel also witnessed the rise of Socialism, Zionism, and Communism, which challenged yeshiva as well as lay youth to examine their philosophies of life and to choose between ideals based on Torah and those formulated by man.

---

[32]Interview with Rabbi Lesin, *op. cit.* See also *Ha-Meliz,* 1897, No. 67. See also Dov Katz, *Tenuath ha-Musar, op. cit.,* III, 43.

[33]See *Ha-Meliz,* 1897, No. 67.

[34]Interview with Rabbi Lesin, *op. cit.* See also Dov Katz, *Tenuath ha-Musar, op. cit.,* III, 44.

Rabbi Finkel realized that a new school of thought, based on Torah and musar, must be developed to stem the tide of the secular movement. He was convinced that a generation of students educated and nurtured in the paths of Torah and musar was the best investment for the preservation of Judaism and the Jewish people.

The Slobodca school is more akin to the Kelm school than to the Navaradock. The basic difference between Kelm and Slobodca was in their approach to the nature of man. Slobodca rejected the ascetic tendencies of Navaradock as well as the more moderate system of Kelm, believing that neither school of thought was conducive to greatness in musar. Rabbi Finkel argued that the Kelm and the Navaradock schools placed too much emphasis on the finiteness and helplessness of man; and this state of mind, he felt, could crush a man's spirit. Instead, his argument went, it was imperative to teach that man is a great being, with unlimited potential for spiritual development.

The Slobodca School of Thought
Introduction

If Rabbi Israel Salanter is the "father" of musar, Rabbi Nathan Zvi Finkel is one of its greatest commentators. Rabbi Finkel in his humility did not desire more than to be just that—a commentator on the teachings of his master. In truth, however, he created new ideas and ideals and added new chapters to musar, which he felt was necessary for the wholeness of Judaism.[35]

His Views on Man

Although Rabbi Finkel was influenced by his teacher, Rabbi Simhah Zissel, nevertheless his critical analysis and thinking produced a school of thought all his own. At the center of this thinking was his high esteem of man in general and the Jew in particular.[36] His view of man differed from that of Rabbi Simhah Zissel, who assumed that only through education and musar would man achieve spiritual and ethical heights. Rabbi Finkel felt that man was born in the image of God, and that it was wrong to assume that only through education and musar would he reach these

---

[35]See Rabbi Jehiel J. Weinberg, "Rabbi Nathan Zvi Finkel" in *Shridei Ash* (Jerusalem, 1969), p. 310. Also see interview with Rabbi Lesin, *op. cit.*
[36]*Ibid.*

heights.[37] Since man was born with a soul, and since the universe was created to serve the purpose of man, it was necessary to recognize God in him. The *acceptance* of man as a spiritual and ethical individual would help him strive to achieve superior qualities. It would enable man to see a lofty purpose and high ideals in his environment.

According to Rabbi Finkel, the human being was endowed with great spiritual powers and must be motivated to recognize and utilize his potential.[38] He held that man's spiritual and physical beings were endowed with a transcendental quality.[39]

Musarites have generally assumed that there is a dichotomy between man's intellect and his emotions and drives. The former emanates from the spirit, the latter from bodily functions.[40] The Slobodca school of musar does not accept this dichotomy, holding that even man's physical emotions and drives are manifestations of the spirit.[41] In order words, a human being—and this refers to the *whole man*—is born in the image of God, and thus has a transcendental link with his Creator.[42]

His Views on Man's Degeneration

In his lectures to his students Rabbi Finkel always emphasized that man at his beginnings was "a creature [formed] by the hands of God," and an inheritor of spiritual and ethical characteristics.[43] Man is the only creature with free will to do good or evil. A woman is endowed with the same spiritual, ethical, and physical qualities as a man, for she was made from man's rib. Since the rib is a hidden limb it symbolizes modesty, which is the particular spiritual quality of a woman.

After Adam and Eve sinned, the lofty attributes of man began to degenerate. As generation after generation continued to sin, man also continued to degrade himself spiritually as well as physically. At the present time man, influenced by materialism and corruption,

---

[37]Interview with Rabbi Lesin, *op. cit.*

[38]*Ibid*. See also Rabbi Weinberg, *op. cit.*

[39]See Abraham S. Finkel, *N'Tivot ha-Musar* (Tel Aviv: A. Tziyoni Publishers, 1961), pp. 26, 48, 165. See also interview with Rabbi Lesin, *op. cit.*

[40]*Ibid.*, pp. 126-133. See also interview with Rabbi Lesin, *op. cit.*

[41]*Ibid*. See also interview with Rabbi Lesin, *op. cit.*

[42]*Ibid*. See also interview with Rabbi Lesin, *op. cit.*

[43]See Rabbi Nathan Zvi Finkel, "Ha-adam V'habhirah" in *Or Ha-Zafon* (Jerusalem, 1968), pp. 206-217.

has become like a wild animal. The world has made remarkable progress in science and technology, but the human conscience has reached a stage of immorality, corruption, and intentional sin. However, despite man's gradual degeneration he has not lost his original image of God. Therefore, in each generation it is possible to regain the lofty attributes with which man was created. Man can in every period of time correct his evil inclinations by doing good, thus regaining the high standards of former generations known for ethics and spirituality. Free will, together with man's creation in the image of God, can elevate man to his former spiritual and ethical heights.[44]

Rabbi Finkel held that the teachings of the Torah were divine, surpassing human reason. According to him, the Torah starts where human reason has left off. In short, man must strive to better himself spiritually and ethically as much as human reason permits him, and after that, the teachings of God must guide him.[45]

His Views on Repentance

It is not the intention of God to inflict hardships upon man in order to exact repentance from him. Man must realize that the path to repentance can be followed by the recognition of God's kindness.[46] Pharaoh failed to recognize the goodness of God, therefore God brought the ten plagues down upon him. In this instance, God appeared to Pharaoh as One Who punished him in order to exact his repentance. According to Rabbi Finkel, wicked persons such as Pharaoh need to have such inflictions visited upon them, because ordinary hardships cannot teach them to repent. Such people forget the goodness of God as soon as their troubles are over.[47]

His Views of Man's Happiness

This world was created so that man could live a life of happiness. If man lives an unhappy life he must blame himself, not God. The purpose of the precepts of the Torah is to bring happiness and bliss to the world and the world hereafter. According to

---

[44]Ibid.
[45]Interview with Rabbi Jacob Lesin, op. cit.
[46]See Rabbi Nathan Zvi Finkel, "Derekh Hatsuvah" in Or Ha-Zafon, op. cit., pp. 28-31.
[47]Ibid.

Rabbi Finkel, the entire creation—as well as man's body—has a transcendental quality. Therefore, one should not reject the wholesome and proper pleasures of life.[48]

His Views on the Spirit of Torah

Rabbi Finkel stressed the importance of study and living in the spirit of Torah. Ethics in the spirit of Torah demand the total absence of tendencies and inclinations toward carrying out evil acts. Ethics in the spirit of God differ from human ethics because they are concerned with the motive and the intent as well as with the roots of an action. The uprooting of devious tendencies in man's nature is the primary purpose of Torah ethics, as compared to human ethics.[49]

The Slobodca School of Thought after Rabbi Finkel's Death

After Rabbi Finkel's death in 1928 the Hebron Yeshiva in Palestine was under the capable leadership of Rabbi Epstein, who arrived from Slobodca that same year. Rabbi Yechazkael Sarna and Rabbi Leib Chasman provided excellent Talmud instruction and inspired the students through creative musar talks and personal involvement in their behalf. After the bloody Arab massacre of 1929, in which fifty-nine students and other Jews were killed, the Hebron Yeshiva moved to Jerusalem. After the deaths of Rabbi Epstein in 1934 and Rabbi Chasman in 1936, Rabbi Sarna headed the yeshiva. At the present time the head of the Hebron Yeshiva is Rabbi Moshe Hebroni, a son-in-law of Rabbi Epstein.[50]

After Rabbi Epstein left for Palestine to head the Hebron Yeshiva, the Slobodca yeshiva Kneseth Israel came under the leadership of Rabbi Isaac Shor and Rabbi Abraham Grodzinski. In 1944 Rabbi Grodzinski, lying in a hospital with a broken leg, died in the fire set in the hospital by the Nazis. Rabbi Shor, who was outside the borders of Lithuania during the destruction of the yeshiva and the massacre of its students, managed to survive and to reach Palestine. In 1945 he broke ground for a new Slobodca Ye-

---

[48]Interview with Rabbi Lesin, op. cit.

[49]Ibid.

[50]See Dov Katz, Tenuath ha-Musar, op. cit., III, 107-109. See also Rabbi Ephraim Ashri, "Slobodca" in Mosdoth Torah B'Europa B'Binyanim U B'Hurbanam, op. cit., pp. 156-160.

shiva in Bnei-Brak. When he died in 1952, he was succeeded as head of the yeshiva by his son-in-law, Rabbi Mordecai Shulman.[51]

There is ample evidence that the Slobodca school of musar is influential in Israel as well as in the United States. Yeshivoth in both countries continue to teach Talmud and musar under roshei yeshivoth who were students of the Slobodca school of musar. Both yeshivoth in Israel were rooted in the teachings of Rabbi Finkel. Both have produced hundreds of scholars who have played important roles in Israel in shaping the religious, ethical, and educational life of Jews there.

In the United States the influence of Rabbi Finkel is considerable. The following distinguished centers of learning followed the Slobodca school of musar: Torah V'Daath, headed by Rabbi Yaakov Kaminetsky; Ner Israel, Baltimore, Md., under Yaakov Ruderman; the Lakewood (N.J.) Yeshiva, under Rabbi Aaron Kotler; Chaim Berlin, under Rabbi Isaac Hutner; Yeshivath Rabbi Israel Meir ha-Kohen, under Rabbi David Levovitz; Yeshivath Mir, under Rabbi Abraham Kalmanowitz; Yeshivath Kamenetz, under Rabbi Naphtali Levovitz, Rabbi Jacob Lesin and Rabbi Avigdor Cyperstein, of Yeshivath Rabbi Isaac Elhanan, and Professor Saul Lieberman, of the Jewish Theological Seminary of America, and others, were students of the Slobodca school of musar.[52]

The Literature of the Slobodca School of Thought

Rabbi Finkel's articles and letters reveal his thoughts and attitudes. *Or Ha-Zafon*, Volumes I-IV, Kovna, 1928-1929, contain primary source material dealing with musar, God-fearing, Judaism, self-recognition, self-analysis, and good traits based upon the Torah. Rabbi Finkel's diary, published in Dov Katz's *Tenuath ha-Musar*, Volume III, contains material which sheds light on his personality as well as his ideas. *Tenuath ha-Musar* itself is an excellent primary source.

Eliezer E. Friedman's articles in *Sefer ha-Zichronoth* and in *Ha-Meliz* (1897) are significant for their coverage of the origin of the Slobodca school. Ephraim Ashri's article on the Slobodca Yeshiva is a scholarly one, since the editor of *Mosdoth Torah B'Europa*

---

[51]*Ibid*. See also Dov Katz, *op. cit.*, pp. 109-111. See also Ephrain Ashri, *op. cit.*, pp. 160-168.

[52]See Dov Katz, *op. cit.*, p. 112f.

B'Binyanim u B'Hurbanam was Professor Samual Mirsky. Jehiel Weinberg's article on Rabbi Finkel in *Shridei Ash* is scholarly and provides valuable information on the man and his school.

Abraham Finkel's *N'Tivot ha-Musar* and Jacob Lesin's *Derekh Hayyim* and *Ha-Maor Sheba-Torah* must be used for an understanding of Rabbi Finkel's school of thought.

A sample of Rabbi Finkel's articles and letters has been translated by the author to show the primary source as well as its value for our times.

Excerpts from Rabbi Finkel's Diary

I must remember to fulfill all my obligations in matters dealing with the study of Torah, God-fearing, and character building. . . . I must remember to seek guidance from the wise without thinking that I am more sagacious than others . . . I must write down immediately the doubts that arise in my mind concerning Judaism and I must resolve them. . . . I must devote time each day to the study of musar and abstain from indulging in gossip and tale-bearing. . . . I must keep all my vows that I made during trying and difficult times.[53]

Highness of Man

Man must strive to be like his Maker and then he will achieve a spiritual highness. If man will attempt to emulate only the materialistic rather than the spiritual attributes that his Creator endowed him with, he will fail to reach the highness of man, namely, that he is born in the image of God. Only through good deeds can one reach the likeness of God in man.[54]

Relationship to Fellow Man

One must at all times be aware of proper respect, tolerance and forms of speech toward one's fellow man. . . . One must restrain oneself under the most difficult conditions from insulting his friend in the presence of others. . . . One must

---

[53]Rabbi Nathan Zvi Finkel, *Diary* in Dov Katz, *op. cit.,* pp. 211-229.
[54]Rabbi Finkel, "Highness of Man" in Dov Katz, *op. cit.,* p. 155.

search every day or at least once a week for ways to help one's friend. . . . Since every Jew is considered a son of a king, one must master the relationships to fellow Jews just as butlers in the palace of a king become experts in the art of catering to their sovereign.[55]

Purpose of Torah Education

Once, followers of the Enlightenment came to visit Rabbi Finkel and asked him the purpose of his way of education. He answered them: "To cultivate wise and good human beings . . . to educate the ignorant to be wise and learned and to change evildoers into men of good will . . . and to provide understanding and enlightenment necessary for good deeds and the proper practice of the precepts of the Torah."[56]

---

[55]Rabbi Finkel, "Relationship to Fellow Man" in Dov Katz, *op. cit.*, pp. 243f.
[56]Rabbi Finkel, "Purpose of Torah Education" in Dov Katz, *op cit.*, p. 207.

CONCLUSION

It is rare in Jewish history for a movement to leave behind it a legacy of great personalities, significant contributions, noble deeds, and great works in rabbinic and ethical literature. The Musar Movement was such a one. It stressed the perfection of Torah, deeds, and the wholeness of the person so that the individual would be well adjusted to God and to his fellow man. It was concerned with several aspects of life: the relationship between God and the world; between nation and man; between the Written Law and the Oral Law. It expressed views on life and death, good and evil, commandment and transgression, and reward and punishment.

There was no situation, no edict, no tribulation of the time which Rabbi Israel Salanter and his disciples did not inquire into and investigate. The men of the Musar Movement sought to understand what the will of God was with regard to them; to discern because of whom and because of what such evil befell their generation, and why the generation was responsible for it. The writings of the Musar Movement contain eternal value, even though they came about as a response to the particular conditions of one particular generation, its contemporary events and its experiences. The Musar Movement sought to give its generation the philosophy of life it needed in order to survive.

Its impact on the dissemination of the teachings of the Torah, on the education of children, and on the establishment and maintenance of yeshivoth is immeasurable. Its contributions to rabbinic literature, human relations, religious and ethical aspects of military life, religious and social problems of immigration, and to various aspects of the political, economic, and social life of Jews, observant and otherwise, are of great importance not only to Jewish history but also to Russian history, particularly in understanding minorities in the Russian Empire.

Morality and religious observance constituted both the reason and the object of the Musar Movement, for it was convinced that

1. Under the conditions of modern times (1810-1945) the continuation of Jewish existence depended on traditional Judaism;

2. Fostering moral and religious consciousness among the Jews in Eastern Europe (Poland and Russia) depended on an inner rededication of the Jewish masses to the study of Torah and the precepts of Judaism and morality;

3. Under contemporary conditions Jewish messianism, based upon the Torah, provided the hope for overcoming the political, economic, military, social, and educational suffering of the exile.

This study tried to show that these ideas recur in the writings of the followers of the Musar Movement and that they represent the underlying motive of Rabbi Israel Salanter and his disciples as active contributors to the life of the Jews in Eastern Europe.

The contributions and impact of Rabbi Salanter and his disciples on their generation must be carefully investigated and analyzed, since our generation—beset by a drug-oriented culture, breakdown of the family unit, lack of moral discipline, and lack of inspiration from spiritual and educational leaders—can benefit immensely from their writings and deeds. If relevance regarding scholarship and deeds is the cry of our generation, certainly Rabbi Salanter and his disciples are an ideal example of men who were concerned with every aspect of life. Their writings remain relevant and meaningful to our times.

In historical perspective, Rabbi Israel Salanter and his followers had the foresight and courage to resist the enlightenment and the assimilation policies of Russian Tsars in order to safeguard the secret of Jewish survival, namely the Torah and its teachings.

BIBLIOGRAPHY

The bibliography in Section *A* includes primary sources. Section *B* deals with secondary sources during the time of the Musar Movement.

A. Primary Sources

Adadawski, Nahum. "Esh Yatzah M'Hesbon" in *Ha-Meliz*, 22, 1890.

American Jewish Year Book. Philadelphia: Jewish Publication Society of America, 1903-1904; 1906-1907.

Amsterdam, Naphtali. In *Or Ha-Musar,* Vols. I, II. Bnai Brak: Hokhma v'Musar, 1965, 1966.

Babli, Hillel. "Rabbi Isaac Blazer," *Bitzaron.* New York: 1928.

Benjamin, Emil. *Rabbi Israel Salant: Sein Leben and Wirken.* Berlin: 1899.

Blazer, Isaac. "Elbonah Shel Torah" in *Ha-Tzfira*, 18, 1890.

—————. *Etz Prei.* Jerusalem: 1903.

—————. In *Or ha-Musar.* Vols. I, II.

—————. *Or Israel.* Vilna: 1900.

Danzig, Abraham. *Chai Adam.* Vilna: 1936.

Elias, Joseph. "Israel Salanter," *Jewish Leaders.* Edited by Leo Jung. Jerusalem: Boys Town Publishing, 1964.

Epstein, Baruch. *Makor Baruch.* Vol. II. Vilna: 1928.

Finkel, Abraham. *N'tivot Ha-Musar.* Tel Aviv: A. Tziyoni Publishers, 1961.

Finkel, Nathan Zvi. *Or Ha-Zafon.* Vols. I-V. Kovna: 1928-1929.

Friedman, Eliezer, E. *Sefer Ha-Zichronoth 1858-1926.* Tel Aviv: 1926.

—————. "Toldoth Baalei Ha-Musar" in *Ha-Meliz*, 111, 1897.

Glenn, M. G. *Israel Salanter: Religious-Ethical Thinker.* New York: Bloch Publishing Co., 1953.

Gordon, Judah. "Binah Le-Toeh Ruah" in *Ha-Meliz*, 4, 1878.

—————. *Iggerot.* Edited by Isaac Jacob. Vols. I, II. Warsaw: Suldberg Bros., 1894.

—————. *Kol Kitbe.* Vol. I.

—————. *Kol Shirei.* Vol. IV, Satire 9.

"Ha-shahar." Vilna: 1880.

Heller, Joshua. *Dibre Joshua.* Vilna: 1886.

—————. *Maoz ha-Dat.* Jerusalem: 1913.

Herzl, Theodor. *Gesammelte Zionistische Werke.* Vols. I-V. Berlin: Judischer Verlag, 1922-23.

—————. *A Jewish State.* Translated by S. D'Avigdor. Second revised edition with a foreword by Israel Cohen. London: 1934.

—————. *Tagebucher.* Edited by Leon Kellner. Vols. I-III. Berlin: Judischer Verlag, 1922-1923.

Hurwitz, Joseph Yozel. *Madragath ha-Adam.* New York: Beth Joseph, 1947.

Kagan, Israel Meir. *Ahavath Hased.* Warsaw: 1888.
————. *Beth Israel.* Petersburg: 1928.
————. *Chomas Hadas.* Petersburg: 1905.
————. *Hafets Hayyim.* Warsaw: 1873.
————. *Mahaneh Israel.* New York: Shulsinger Bros., 1943.
————. *Michtavei Hafets Hayyim.* Edited and introduction by Ariah Leib Kagan. New York: Saphrograph, 1953.
————. *Nidhei Israel.* Warsaw: 1893.
————. *Shem Olam.* Warsaw: 1893.
————. *Torah Habaith.* Petersburg: 1907.
————. "Kosher Essen Far Yuddish Zelner," *Der Jud.* LXIV.
Katz, Dov. *Tenuath ha-Musar.* Tel Aviv: Baitan ha-Sefer, 1952-1963. 5 Vols.
Katznelson, Benjamin. "Rabbi Isaac Blazer," *Ha-Tzfira.* Warsaw: 1900. No. 82.
————. "Kol Yaakov" in *Ha-Tzfira,* 18, 1870.
————. "Kol Yaakov" in *Ha-Tzfira,* 81, 1900.
Lenin, Vladimer. Sochineniia, second edition XXIV, 1932, 203.
"Letter from Russian Jews in England to Pobedonostsev" in *Sichron Jacob.* Vol. III. 70-76.
Levin, Moses. "Nazir Israel," *Ha-Meliz,* 1883. No. 18.
Lilienblum, M. L. *Kol Kitbe,* Vol. III.
————. "Orhot Ha-Talmud" in *Kol Kitbe Moses Leib Lilienblum.* Cracow: Joseph Fisher Publishers, 1910.
————. "Nefesh Tahahth Nefesh" in *Ha-Meliz,* 4, 1878.
Lipschitz, Jacob. *Sichron Jacob.* Vols. I-III. Kovna: 1927, 1930.
Lutzevski, Naphtali Herz Leib. "Haskafah al Matzav Achenu Bnei Israel Ha-Homri V'Ha-Musari" in *Ha-Maggid,* 7, 1874.
Mark, Jacob. *Gdolim Fun Unser Tseit.* New York: 1927.
Mirsky, Samuel K. *Mosdoth Torah B'Europa B'binyanam U'vehurbanam.* New York: Egan Press, 1956.
Nekritz, Y. L. "Yeshivath Navaradock — Beth Joseph." New York: 1956.
Pobedonostsev, Constantine. "The Jews" in *Ha-Meliz,* 18, 1882.
Rosenfeld, S. *Rabbi Israel Salanter.* Warsaw: 1911.
Salanter, Israel. "Ma-orer Ha-Nirtamin" in *Ha-Meliz,* 8, 1879.
————. *Igeret ha-Musar.* Edited by Isaac Blazer in *Or Israel.* Vilna: 1900.
————. In *Or ha-Musar.* Vols. I, II.
Sharfstein, Zvi. "Rabbi Israel Salanter, The Father of the Musar Movement," *Ha-Doar.* New York: 1962. No. 12.
————. "Bntivoth ha-Musar," *Ha-Doar.* New York: 1962. No. 6.
Sokolow, Nahum. "Ha-Tzfira." Warshaw: 1931.
Steinschneider, Maggid. *Ir Vilna.* Vilna: 1900.
Tarsis, Zelig. *Ein Tarsis.* Vol. I. Jerusalem: 1940.
Weinberg, Jehiel J. *Shridei Ash.* Jerusalem: 1969.
Yeshivath Navaradock. *Or ha-Musar.* Vols. I, II. Bnai Brak: Hokhma v'Musar, 1965, 1966.

Yosher, Moses M. "Israel Meir Ha-Kohen—Hafets Hayyim," *Jewish Leaders*. Edited by Leo Jung. Jerusalem: Boys Town Jerusalem Publishers, 1964.

Zissel, Simcha. *Hokhma-Umesar*. Copyright by Simcho Ziesel Levovitz. Vols. I, II. New York: Aber Press, Inc. 1957, 1964.

—————. In *Or ha-Musar*. Vols. I, II.

—————. "Tvunah." Jerusalem: 1941. No. II.

B. SECONDARY SOURCES

"Alexander III," *Evreiskaia Enciclopedia*. I (1906), 825-839.

Baron, Salo W. *The Russian Jews: Under Tsars and Soviets*. New York: Macmillan Co., 1964.

Curtiss, J. S. "The Army of Nicholas I: Its Role and Character," *American Historical Review*, LXIII (1958).

Dubnow, Simon M. History of the Jews in Russia and Poland. 3 vols. Trans. by I. Friedlaender. Philadelphia: Jewish Publication Society of America, 1946.

—————. *Veltgeshikhe fun Yiddishn Folk* (World History of the Jewish People). 10 vols. Buenos Aires-New York: 1956.

Elbogen, Ismar. *A Century of Jewish Life*. Trans. from the German by Moses Hadas. Philadelphia: Jewish Publication Society of America, 1946.

Fadiev, Rostislav A. *Vooruzhennia Silly Rossii* (Russian Army). Moscow: 1968.

Florinsky, Michael T. *Russia: A History and an Interpretation*. 2 vols. New York: Macmillan Co., 1964.

Frederic, Harold. *The New Exodus: A Study of Israel in Russia*. London 1892.

Fuenn, S. M. "Pirhe Tsafon" (Flowers of the North). Vila: 1853-1875.

Graetz, Heinrich. *Geschichte der Juden* (History of the Jews). 11 vols. 1853-1875.

Gershenzon, M. O. Ed. *Epokha Nikolaia I.* (Epoch of Nichols I). Moscow: 1911.

Ginsburg, Saul M. *Historishe Werk*. 3 vols. New York: 1937.

Glenn, M. G. *Israel Salanter: Religious-Ethical Thinker*. New York: Bloch Publishing Co., 1953.

Glinoetskii, Nikolai P. *Istoriia Russkago Generalnago Shtabe* (History of the Russian General Staff). St. Petersburg: 1888-1894.

Greenberg, Louis. *The Jews in Russia*. New Haven: Yale University Press, 1965.

Grodzenski, Ozer. "Kneseth Israel" (Gathering of Israel). Slobodca: 1939-1940.

Herzen, Alexander. *Byloe i Dumy* (My Past and Thoughts). 6 vols. London: Chatto and Windus, 1924-1927.

Heilperin, I. Ed. *Bet Yisrael B'Polin* (The Jewish People in Poland). 2 vols. Jerusalem: 1948.

Jung, Leo. Ed. *Jewish Leaders*. Jerusalem: Boys Town Jerusalem Publishers, 1964.

Karpovich, Michael. *Imperial Russia, 1801-1917.*. New York: H. Holt, 1932.

Kliuchevsky, V. O. *Kurs Russkoi Istorii* (Course of Russian History). 5 vols. Petrograd: 1918-1921.

Kornilov, A. A. *Kurs Istorri v XIX veke* (Course of Russian History During the Nineteenth Century). 3 vols. Moscow: 1912-1914.

Levinsohn, Isaac Baer. *Bet Yehuda* (House of Judah). Vilna: 1839.

――――. *Te'udah b'Israel* (Instruction in Israel). Vilna: 1828.

Mahler, Raphael. *Geshichte fun Yidn in Polyn, Letste Yor Hundeter* (Jewish History in Poland, Last Centuries). New York: 1957.

――――. *Ha-Hasiduth v'Haskalah* (Hasidism and Enlightenment). Marhavia: 1961.

Maimonides, Moses. *Eight Chapters.*

Ovsi, Joshua. *Articles and Notes.* New York: 1947.

Phillipson, David. *Max Lilienthal.* New York: 1915.

Pobedonostsev, K.P. *Reflections of a Russian Statesman.* London: 1898.

Polievktov, Mikhail. *Nikolai I Biografia i Obzer Tsarstvovaniia.* St. Petersburg: 1914.

Pomerantz, Gedaliah. "Memoirs of the World War I," *Ha-Doar.* No. 15. New York: February 8, 1963.

Rabinovitz, Reuben. "The City is Burning," *Ha-Doar.* No. 18, New York: March 2, 1962.

Raisin, Jacob B. *The Haskalah Movement in Russia.* Philadelphia: Jewish Publication Society of America, 1913.

Reddaway, W. F. *Cambridge History of Poland.* Cambridge University Press, 1950.

Rhine, Abraham. *Leon Gordon.* Philadelphia: Jewish Publication Society of America, 1910.

Rivkind, Isaac. "Rabbi Isaac Elhanan," *Ha-Doar.* New York: April 13, 1962.

Robinson, Edward. *Biblical Researches in Palestine.* Boston: 1841.

Sachs, A. S. *Studies in Jewish Biobliography in Memory of A. S. Freidus.* New York: 1925.

Schapiro, Leonard. *The Communist Party of the Soviet Union.* New York: Vintage Books, 1964.

Schapiro, M. S. "Rabbi Naphtali Zvi Berlin," *Ha-Doar.* New York: June 22, 1962.

Seton Watson, Hugh. *The Decline of Imperial Russia, 1885-1919.* New York: Praeger, 1956.

Sokolow, Nahum, *History of Zionism, 1600-1918.* With an introduction by A. J. Balfour. Vol. II. London: Longmans, 1919.

Treadgold, Donald. *Twentieth Century Russia.* Chicago: Rand McNally, 1959.

Venturi, Franco. *Roots of Revolution: A History of the Populist and Socialist Movements in the Nineteenth Century.* Introduction by Isiah Berlin. New York: Knopf, 1960.

Witte, Sergei. *The Memoirs of Count Witte.* Trans. from the Russian and edited by Abraham Yarmolinsky. New York: Doubleday, 1921.

INDEX